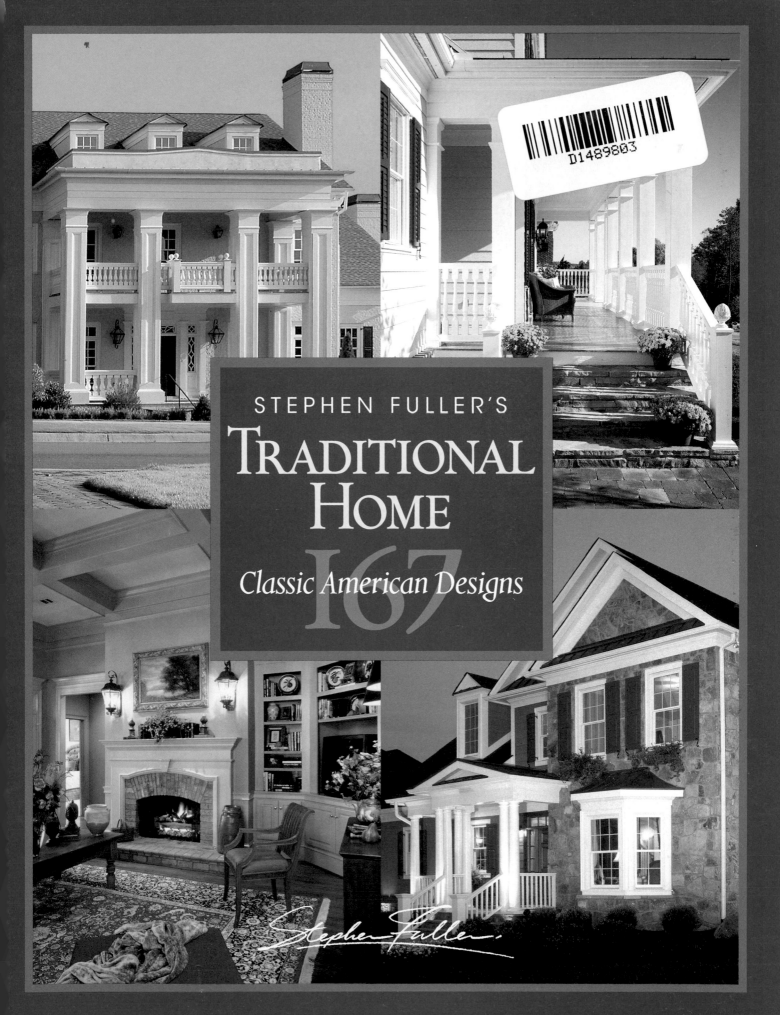

STEPHEN FULLER'S

TRADITIONAL HOME

167

Classic American Designs

Stephen Fuller

STEPHEN FULLER'S
TRADITIONAL HOME

Published by Hanley Wood
One Thomas Circle, NW, Suite 600
Washington, DC 20005

General Manager, Plans Services, David Rook
Associate Publisher, Development, Jennifer Pearce
Manager, Customer Service, Michael Morgan
Director, Marketing, Mark Wilkin
Editor, Simon Hyoun
Assistant Editor, Kimberly R. Griffin
Publications Manager, Brian Haefs
Production Manager, Theresa Emerson
Senior Plan Merchandiser, Nicole Phipps
Plan Merchandiser, Hillary Gottemoeller
Graphic Artist, Joong Min
Manager, Plans & Web Operations, Susan Jasmin
Director, Audience Development, Erik Schulze

Hanley Wood Corporate
Chief Executive Officer, Frank Anton
Chief Financial Officer, Matthew Flynn
Chief Administrative Officer, Frederick Moses
Chief Information Officer, Jeffrey Craig
Executive Vice President/Corporate Sales, Ken Beach
Vice President/Finance, Brad Lough
Vice President/Legal, Mike Bender
Interim Vice President/Human Resources, Bill McGrath

Most Hanley Wood titles are available at quantity discounts with bulk purchases for educational, business, or sales promotional use. For information, please contact Jennifer Pearce at jpearce@hanleywood.com.

VC Graphics, Inc.
Creative Director, Veronica Vannoy
Graphic Designer, Jennifer Gerstein
Graphic Designer, Denise Reiffenstein
Graphic Designer, Jeanne-Erin Worster

PHOTO CREDITS
Front Cover, Top Left: Design HPK3600153, for details see page 167, photo courtesy of Stephen Fuller, Inc. Top Right: Design HPK3600064, for details see page 72, photo by Scott W. Moore. Bottom Right: Design HPK3600065, for details see page 76, photo courtesy of Stephen Fuller, Inc. Bottom Left, Back Cover Main: Design HPK3600001, for details see page 6, photo by B. Massey Photographers, courtesy of Stephen Fuller, Inc. Back Cover Inset: Design HPK3600135, for details see page 146, Photo by B. Massey Photographers.

Distribution Center
PBD
Hanley Wood Consumer Group
3280 Summit Ridge Parkway
Duluth, Georgia 30096

10 9 8 7 6 5 4 3 2 1

Printed in the United States of America

Library of Congress Control Number: 2007930104

ISBN-13: 978-1-931131-79-7
ISBN-10: 1-931131-79-1

centered at the rear of the family room. The wide-open interior is also an invitation to natural light, which enters by way of the sunroom, carefully placed skylights, and a set of French doors leading out to a side deck and pool area. Overnight guests will find privacy and convenience in the second bedroom, which splits a bath with

the nearby office; separate vanities and a compartmented bath make sharing easy.

Complementing the home's good manners is a perfectly planned kitchen that indulges a family's casual spirit. The breakfast nook and island kitchen provide spaces for everyday dining. The nearby second entry helps to employ

ABOVE: A modest pool complements the rear elevation and leaves room on the lot for other features.

the utility areas and the garage to everyday kitchen chores, such as bringing in groceries from the car or stocking the pantry. The side deck, with access to a half-bath and bar areas, is an ideal space for outdoor dining.

Finally, the master suite provides a replenishing retreat from a long day of work and play. The bedroom features a decorative tray ceiling, panoramic views to the side of the plan, and private access to the deck. The master bath delivers a long list of amenities—dual vanities, whirlpool tub, compartmented toilet, steam shower—and is attended by a very generous walk-in closet. A brief entryway serves to separate and secure the space for the fortunate homeowners.

ABOVE: Family dining is bright and comfortable in the well-lit breakfast area.

HPK3600001

Square Footage: 2,752
Bedrooms: 3
Bathrooms: 2 ½
Width: 90' - 0"
Depth: 72' - 10"
Foundation: Unfinished Basement
Price Code: C4

Order online @ eplans.com

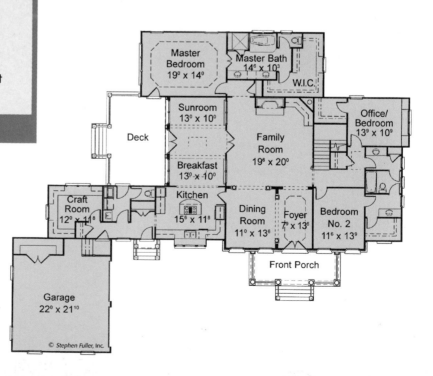

BELOW: Built-in shelves, a coffered ceiling, and a centerpiece
fireplace suggest formal tones in the family room.

© Stephen Fuller, Inc.

HPK3600002

First Floor: 1,580 sq. ft.
Second Floor: 595 sq. ft.
Total: 2,175 sq. ft.
Bedrooms: 3
Bathrooms: 2 ½
Width: 48' - 0"
Depth: 69' - 6"
Foundation: Finished
Walkout Basement
Price Code: C4

Order online @ eplans.com

AZALEA HILL

Traditional formality asks for well-defined rooms, while the demands of sophisticated lifestyles call for wide-open spaces that bend to patterns of living. The formal dining room opens through decorative pillars to the two-story great room, which features a fireplace. French doors lead from the bayed breakfast area to the private master suite, a retreat with a lavish bath featuring an angled whirlpool tub, glass-enclosed shower, and twin vanities. Two family bedrooms share a bath upstairs.

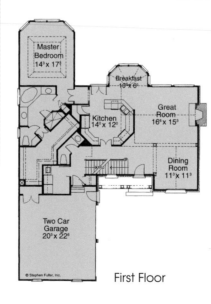
First Floor

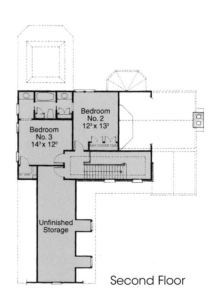
Second Floor

ACORN HILL

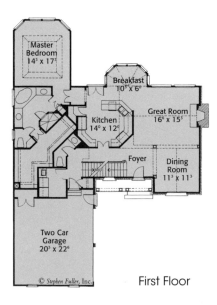

Master Bedroom 14³ x 17³

Breakfast 10⁸ x 6⁰

Great Room 16⁸ x 15⁵

Kitchen 14⁰ x 12⁰

Foyer

Dining Room 11³ x 11³

Two Car Garage 20³ x 22⁶

© Stephen Fuller, Inc.

First Floor

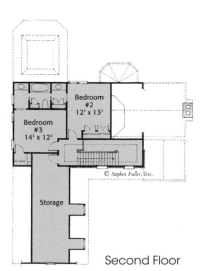

Bedroom #2 12³ x 13³

Bedroom #3 14³ x 12⁰

© Stephen Fuller, Inc.

Storage

Second Floor

HPK3600003

First Floor: 1,580 sq. ft.
Second Floor: 595 sq. ft.
Total: 2,175 sq. ft.
Bedrooms: 3
Bathrooms: 2 ½
Width: 50' - 0"
Depth: 69' - 9"
Foundation: Unfinished
Walkout Basement
Price Code: C4

Order online @ eplans.com

This compact footprint and motor court-style garage make this home ideal for the smallest of lots and a liberal use of angled walls on the first floor make it interesting from every view. The dining and great rooms are separated only by columns and feature dramatic vaulted ceilings. Off the window-lined breakfast area is a large kitchen. In the rear of the home, the master suite includes a garden bath. The second floor houses two additional bedrooms with a shared bath. Storage space or a fourth bedroom may be placed over the garage area.

© Stephen Fuller

HPK3600004

First Floor: 1,652 sq. ft.
Second Floor: 543 sq. ft.
Total: 2,195 sq. ft.
Bonus Space: 470 sq. ft.
Bedrooms: 4
Bathrooms: 3 ½
Width: 46' - 6"
Depth: 72' - 0"
Foundation: Unfinished Basement
Price Code: C4

Order online @ eplans.com

HILLCREST

This stately brick home features a recessed entry and windows topped by a keystone accent. A paneled door crowned by a fanlight opens to an entry hall. Double doors open to a versatile room that serves as either a study with built-in bookshelves or a formal dining room. The great room provides built-ins as well as a fireplace. An island kitchen adjoins a breakfast/sunroom with access to the rear deck. The master suite, thoughtfully secluded, has a spacious bath with two walk-in closets and separate vanities.

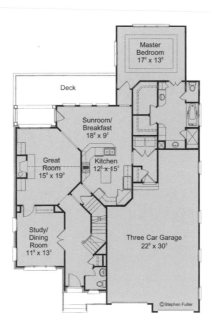

First Floor

Second Floor

© Stephen Fuller, Inc.

BROOKDALE

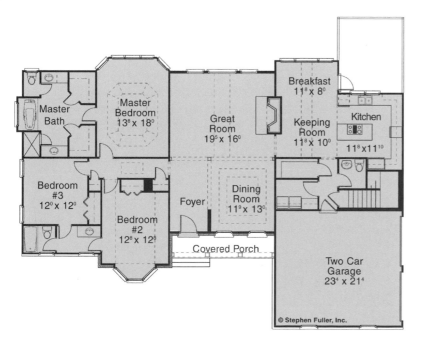

Master Bath

Master Bedroom
13⁸ x 18⁰

Great Room
19⁵ x 16⁰

Breakfast
11⁸ x 8⁰

Keeping Room
11⁸ x 10⁰

Kitchen
11⁸ x 11¹⁰

Bedroom #3
12⁰ x 12⁰

Foyer

Dining Room
11⁹ x 13⁰

Bedroom #2
12⁸ x 12⁸

Covered Porch

Two Car Garage
23⁴ x 21⁴

© Stephen Fuller, Inc.

HPK3600005

Square Footage: 2,204
Bedrooms: 3
Bathrooms: 2 ½
Width: 71' - 2"
Depth: 49' - 7"
Foundation: Finished Walkout Basement
Price Code: C4

Order online @ eplans.com

A bay window is accented by a gracefully covered porch on this three-bedroom home. The large U-shaped kitchen is sure to please, with a work island, plenty of counter and cabinet space, and an adjacent breakfast room. Two secondary bedrooms— one with a bay window—share a full bath. The master suite is full of amenities, such as twin walk-in closets, a water closet, and two vanities.

© Stephen Fuller, Inc.

HPK3600006

First Floor: 1,165 sq. ft.
Second Floor: 1,050 sq. ft.
Total: 2,215 sq. ft.
Bonus Space: 265 sq. ft.
Bedrooms: 3
Bathrooms: 2 ½
Width: 58' - 0"
Depth: 36' - 0"
Foundation: Finished
Walkout Basement
Price Code: C4

Order online @ eplans.com

WESTOVER COMMONS

First Floor

Classic design knows no boundaries in this gracious two-story home. From the formal living and dining areas to the more casual family room, it handles any occasion with ease. A central fireplace provides a focal point in the family room. Of special note on the first floor are the L-shaped kitchen with attached breakfast area and the pampering half-bath.

Second Floor

CARDIFF

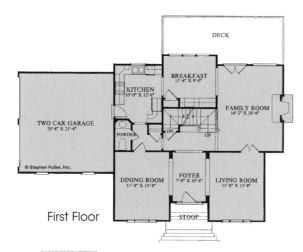

DECK

BREAKFAST
11'-4" X 9'-0"

KITCHEN
10'-0" X 12'-6"

FAMILY ROOM
14'-2" X 18'-4"

TWO CAR GARAGE
20'-8" X 21'-4"

POWDER

DN

UP

© Stephen Fuller, Inc.

DINING ROOM
11'-8" X 13'-8"

FOYER
7'-0" X 10'-6"

LIVING ROOM
11'-8" X 13'-8"

STOOP

First Floor

W.I.C.

MASTER BATH

MASTER BEDROOM
14'-2" X 16'-2"

FUTURE BATH

FUTURE BEDROOM NO. 4
14'-4" X 12'-0"

LAUNDRY

DN

BEDROOM NO. 3
11'-8" X 13'-8"

BATH

BEDROOM NO. 2
11'-8" X 13'-8"

Second Floor

HPK3600007

First Floor: 1,165 sq. ft.
Second Floor: 1,050 sq. ft.
Total: 2,215 sq. ft.
Bonus Space: 265 sq. ft.
Bedrooms: 3
Bathrooms: 2 ½
Width: 58' - 0"
Depth: 36' - 0"
Foundation: Finished
Walkout Basement
Price Code: C4

Order online @ eplans.com

This beautiful European-styled stucco home puts luxury features into only 2,215 square feet. The main living areas are found on the first floor: formal living and dining rooms flanking the entry foyer; a family room with a fireplace; and an L-shaped kitchen with an attached breakfast room. The second-floor master bedroom is a real treat, with a tray ceiling and a thoughtfully appointed bath. Bedrooms 2 and 3 share a full bath with a double-bowl vanity.

HPK3600008

First Floor: 1,104 sq. ft.
Second Floor: 1,144 sq. ft.
Total: 2,248 sq. ft.
Bonus Space: 242 sq. ft.
Bedrooms: 3
Bathrooms: 3
Width: 62' - 6"
Depth: 32' - 0"
Foundation: Unfinished Basement
Price Code: C4

Order online @ eplans.com

ROE HAMPTON PLACE

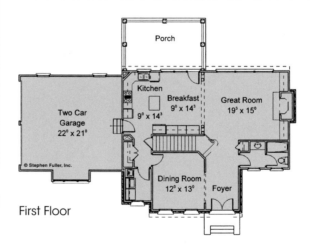

First Floor

This beautiful home features an overhanging second floor with dramatic drop pendants. Inside, the foyer shows gorgeous interior vistas past the staircase to the open great room, which sports a fireplace and plenty of windows for pleasant backyard views. Upstairs, the master suite provides lovely views to the backyard. Two additional bedrooms, a study alcove, and a bonus room provide additional space.

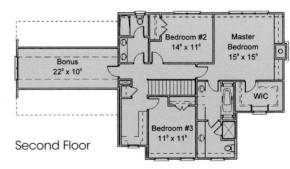

Second Floor

© Stephen Fuller, Inc.

Quincy Hall

DECK

BREAKFAST
12'-0" X 10'-0"

MASTER
BATH

MASTER BEDROOM
13'-0" X 15'-4"

TWO STORY
FAMILY ROOM
14'-6" X 15'-0"

KITCHEN
12'-0" X 14'-8"

POWDER

W.I.C.

DN.

STORAGE

LAUNDRY

DINING ROOM
13'-4" X 11'-8"

TWO STORY
FOYER
9'-0" X 15'-0"

UP

TWO CAR GARAGE
22'-4" X 20'-8"

LIVING ROOM
13'-4" X 11'-4"

STOOP

© Stephen Fuller, Inc.

First Floor

OPEN TO BELOW

BEDROOM NO. 3
11'-10" X 12'-0"

BATH

FUTURE
BEDROOM NO. 4
13'-6" X 12'-0"

DN.

BALCONY

FUTURE
BATH

BEDROOM
NO. 2
13'-0" X 12'-0"

OPEN TO
BELOW

FUTURE
STORAGE

Second Floor

HPK3600009

First Floor: 1,720 sq. ft.
Second Floor: 545 sq. ft.
Total: 2,265 sq. ft.
Bonus Space: 365 sq. ft.
Bedrooms: 3
Bathrooms: 2 ½
Width: 50' - 0"
Depth: 53' - 6"
Foundation: Finished
Walkout Basement
Price Code: C4

Order online @ eplans.com

Style abounds in this English country cottage. Accented by a fireplace and built-in bookcases, the family room is an excellent setting for family gatherings. The central staircase leads to the balcony overlook and a bath serving two family bedrooms. Another bedroom and bath on this level can be completed later.

© Stephen Fuller, Inc.

HPK3600010

First Floor: 1,720 sq. ft.
Second Floor: 545 sq. ft.
Total: 2,265 sq. ft.
Bonus Space: 365 sq. ft.
Bedrooms: 3
Bathrooms: 2 ½
Width: 50' - 0"
Depth: 53' - 6"
Foundation: Finished
Walkout Basement
Price Code: C4

Order online @ eplans.com

CLANDON

First Floor

Second Floor

This French Country cottage is a charming example of European architecture. A two-story foyer opens to an impressive two-story family room with a fireplace. To the right, a formal living area opens to a dining room through decorative columns, which is easily served by a kitchen with island cooktop counter. The master suite is well appointed with a coffered ceiling, walk-in closet, and double-bowl vanity in the bath. The second floor holds two family bedrooms, a full bath, and space for an additional bedroom and future bath.

DAVENPORT COTTAGE

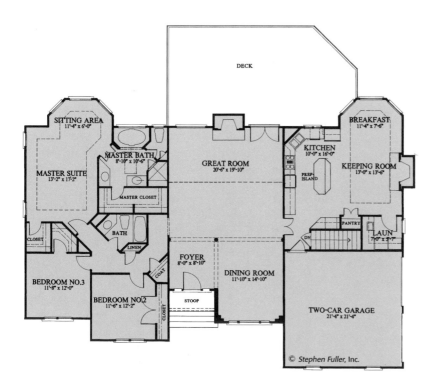

© Stephen Fuller, Inc.

DECK

SITTING AREA
11'-4" x 6'-0"

MASTER BATH
8'-10" x 10'-6"

MASTER SUITE
13'-2" x 17'-2"

MASTER CLOSET

GREAT ROOM
20'-6" x 19'-10"

KITCHEN
10'-0" x 16'-0"

BREAKFAST
11'-4" x 7'-6"

KEEPING ROOM
13'-0" x 13'-6"

PREP-ISLAND

PANTRY

LAUN
7'-0" x 5'-7"

CLOSET

BATH

LINEN

DN

BEDROOM NO.3
11'-8" x 12'-0"

COAT

FOYER
8'-0" x 8'-10"

DINING ROOM
11'-10" x 14'-10"

BEDROOM NO.2
11'-6" x 12'-2"

CLOSET

STOOP

TWO-CAR GARAGE
21'-4" x 21'-4"

HPK3600011

Square Footage: 2,295
Bedrooms: 3
Bathrooms: 2
Width: 69' - 0"
Depth: 49' - 6"
Foundation: Unfinished
Walkout Basement
Price Code: C4

Order online @ eplans.com

The abundance of details in this plan makes it the finest in one-story living. The great room and formal dining room have an open, dramatic sense of space. The kitchen with a preparation island shares the right side of the plan with a bayed breakfast area and a keeping room with a fireplace. Sleeping accommodations to the left of the plan include a master suite and two family bedrooms.

© Stephen Fuller, Inc.

HPK3600012

First Floor: 1,660 sq. ft.
Second Floor: 665 sq. ft.
Total: 2,325 sq. ft.
Bonus Space: 240 sq. ft.
Bedrooms: 3
Bathrooms: 3 ½
Width: 64' - 0"
Depth: 48' - 6"
Foundation: Finished
Walkout Basement
Price Code: C4

Order online @ eplans.com

BANFIELD HALL

First Floor

Second Floor

Stately brick and Jack-arch detailing create an exterior that looks established and possesses a floor plan that offers 21st-Century livability. A dramatic two-story entry is framed by formal living and dining areas. The breakfast nook allows rear covered-porch access and opens to the kitchen. A coffered ceiling, sumptuous bath, and walk-in closet highlight the master suite. Upstairs, two additional bedrooms, an optional fourth bedroom, and two baths complete the plan.

© Stephen Fuller, Inc.

HPK3600013

First Floor: 1,660 sq. ft.
Second Floor: 665 sq. ft.
Total: 2,325 sq. ft.
Bonus Space: 240 sq. ft.
Bedrooms: 3
Bathrooms: 3 ½
Width: 64' - 0"
Depth: 48' - 6"
Foundation: Finished
Walkout Basement
Price Code: C4

Order online @ eplans.com

DUNNING

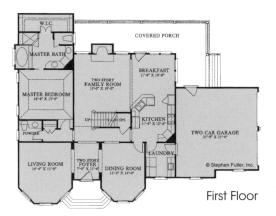

First Floor

Second Floor

This European design is filled with space for formal and informal occasions. Informal areas include an open kitchen, breakfast room and family room with a fireplace. Formal rooms surround the foyer, with the living room on the left and dining room on the right. The master suite is conveniently placed on the first floor, with a gorgeous private bath and a walk-in closet.

© Stephen Fuller, Inc.

HPK3600014

Square Footage: 2,325
Bedrooms: 3
Bathrooms: 2 ½
Width: 66' - 3"
Depth: 74' - 0"
Foundation: Unfinished
Walkout Basement
Price Code: C4

Order online @ eplans.com

RICHMOND

An attractive exterior of wood and stone complements a steeply pitched, dormered roof. The shutters and wood trim add Colonial touches. The foyer opens to the formal dining room. The great room features a vaulted ceiling with a fireplace, wet bar, and built-in cabinets. The master suite connects with the breakfast area/sunroom. Bedrooms on the opposite side of the house feature a Jack-and-Jill bathroom.

Deck

Breakfast/Sunroom
23^0 x 10^0

Bedroom #3
13^0 x 12^0

Great Room
15^6 x 16^0

Kitchen
13^0 x 16^0

Master Bedroom
15^0 x 14^9

Bedroom #2
13^0 x 12^0

Dining Room
13^0 x 10^6

Porch

Storage
13^6 x 7^0

2-Car Garage
21^6 x 25^0

© Stephen Fuller, Inc.

© Stephen Fuller, Inc.

BYRDS RETREAT

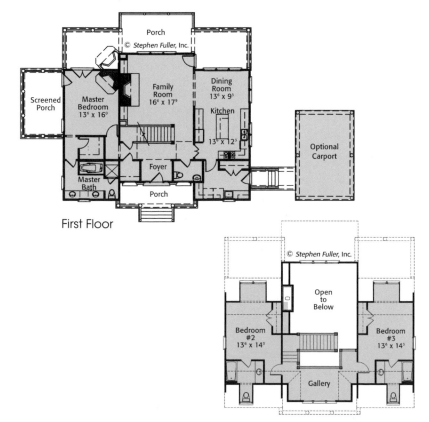

First Floor

Second Floor

HPK3600015

First Floor: 1,470 sq. ft.
Second Floor: 862 sq. ft.
Total: 2,332 sq. ft.
Bedrooms: 3
Bathrooms: 3 ½
Width: 46' - 0"
Depth: 49' - 0"
Foundation: Crawlspace
Price Code: C4

Order online @ eplans.com

This mountain home is simple yet intriguing, and nothing if not perfect for a weekend retreat or second home. Stone, clapboard, and board-and-batten siding provide the finishing touches, and there are numerous outdoor spaces for enjoying views and entertaining. A large fireplace in the family room provides warmth, and a kitchen/dining room make conversation between cook and kin easy. The master suite is well-appointed with a private fireplace and covered porch. Upstairs, two bedrooms have private baths. A rustic but stylish carport is an added bonus.

© Stephen Fuller, Inc.

HPK3600016

Square Footage: 2,377
Bedrooms: 3
Bathrooms: 2
Width: 69' - 0"
Depth: 49' - 6"
Foundation: Finished
Walkout Basement
Price Code: C4

Order online @ eplans.com

TEN BROECK MANOR

One-story living takes a lovely traditional turn in this brick home. The entry foyer opens to the formal dining room and the great room through graceful columned archways. The open gourmet kitchen, bayed breakfast nook, and keeping room with a fireplace will be a magnet for family activity. Sleeping quarters offer two family bedrooms and a hall bath and a rambling master suite with a bayed sitting area and a sensuous bath.

© Stephen Fuller, Inc.

SIERRA

First Floor

Second Floor

HPK3600017

First Floor: 1,156 sq. ft.
Second Floor: 1,239 sq. ft.
Total: 2,395 sq. ft.
Bedrooms: 4
Bathrooms: 2 ½
Width: 57' - 3"
Depth: 39' - 0"
Foundation: Finished
Walkout Basement
Price Code: C4

Order online @ eplans.com

This traditional home combines an attractive, classic exterior with an open and sophisticated interior design. Enter the kitchen from the dining room through a corner butler's pantry for added convenience while entertaining. The open foyer staircase leads to the upper level, beginning with the master suite. The master bath contains a luxurious tub, separate shower and dual vanities, as well as a large linen closet. All three secondary bedrooms share a hall bath that includes a separate vanity and bathing area.

© Stephen Fuller, Inc.

HPK3600018

First Floor: 1,724 sq. ft.
Second Floor: 700 sq. ft.
Total: 2,424 sq. ft.
Bedrooms: 3
Bathrooms: 2 ½
Width: 47' - 10"
Depth: 63' - 8"
Foundation: Finished
Walkout Basement
Price Code: C4

Order online @ eplans.com

All the charm of gables, stonework, and multilevel rooflines combine to create this home. To the left of the foyer, you will see the dining room highlighted by a tray ceiling and expansive windows with transoms. The gourmet kitchen holds a work island, oversized pantry, and adjoining octagonal breakfast room. The great room features a pass-through wet bar, a fireplace, and bookcases. The master suite enjoys privacy at the rear of the home. An open-rail loft above the foyer leads to two additional bedrooms.

DOGWOOD WAY

© Stephen Fuller

First Floor

Second Floor

© Stephen Fuller, Inc.

ROCKSPRINGS JUNCTION

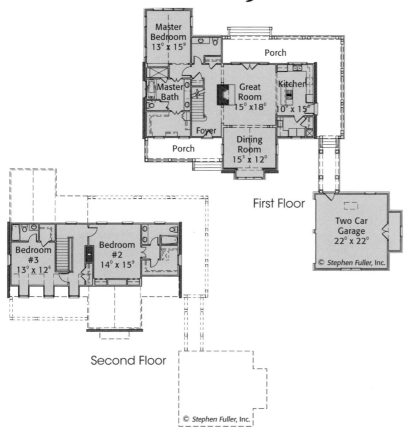

Master Bedroom
13⁰ x 15⁹

Porch

Master Bath

Great Room
15⁰ x18⁰

Kitchen
10⁰ x 15⁹

Foyer

Porch

Dining Room
15³ x 12⁰

First Floor

Two Car Garage
22⁰ x 22⁰

© Stephen Fuller, Inc.

Bedroom #3
13⁰ x 12⁶

Bedroom #2
14⁰ x 15⁹

Second Floor

© Stephen Fuller, Inc.

HPK3600019

First Floor: 1,569 sq. ft.
Second Floor: 879 sq. ft.
Total: 2,448 sq. ft.
Bedrooms: 3
Bathrooms: 3 ½
Width: 76' - 3"
Depth: 77' - 0"
Foundation: Crawlspace
Price Code: C4

Order online @ eplans.com

Fieldstone and reverse board and batten create a rustic exterior that blends with its surroundings. Inside, social spaces work together. A central stone fireplace separates the entrance hall from the great room, where French doors frame a view of a wrap-around porch. The great room flows into a dramatic dining room, where a stone wall reaching the vaulted ceiling frames a bayed seating area. A separate vestibule leads to a roomy downstairs master suite. Two additional bedrooms upstairs feature private baths and walk-in closets.

© Stephen Fuller, Inc.

HPK3600020

First Floor: 1,831 sq. ft.
Second Floor: 651 sq. ft.
Total: 2,482 sq. ft.
Bonus Space: 394 sq. ft.
Bedrooms: 3
Bathrooms: 2 ½
Width: 55' - 0"
Depth: 77' - 0"
Foundation: Finished
Walkout Basement
Price Code: C4

Order online @ eplans.com

This beautiful country home characterizes all the charm of a rural lifestyle. From the covered entrance, the front door opens to a formal dining room and great room with a fireplace. A rear porch offers outdoor livability to the great room. The U-shaped kitchen and adjoining breakfast room are nearby for casual eating. Located on the first floor for privacy, the master suite features two walk-in closets and a bath designed for relaxation. Two family bedrooms with walk-in closets are upstairs.

BRADFORD COURT

First Floor

Second Floor

© Stephen Fuller, Inc.

COTTONWOOD HOMESTEAD

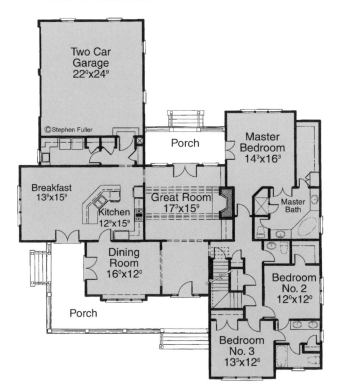

Two Car Garage 22⁰x24⁹

© Stephen Fuller

Porch

Master Bedroom 14³x16³

Breakfast 13⁶x15⁹

Kitchen 12⁰x15⁹

Great Room 17³x15⁹

Master Bath

Dining Room 16⁰x12⁰

Bedroom No. 2 12⁰x12⁰

Porch

Bedroom No. 3 13³x12⁶

HPK3600021

Square Footage: 2,485
Bedrooms: 3
Bathrooms: 2 ½
Width: 64' - 9"
Depth: 78' - 9"
Foundation: Finished
Walkout Basement
Price Code: C4

Order online @ eplans.com

Wood siding and a wraparound porch give this Early American adaptation a warm, inviting quality. The foyer opens to the formal dining room and the great room, where a fireplace and French doors to the rear porch are highlights. The kitchen has a fantastic, angled island and a spacious breakfast room with French doors to the porch. Two family bedrooms that share a private bath balance the large master suite. An extra wide, side-wrap porch with three entrances enlivens the front of this home.

© Stephen Fuller, Inc.

HPK3600022

First Floor: 1,606 sq. ft.
Second Floor: 902 sq. ft.
Total: 2,508 sq. ft.
Bonus Space: 376 sq. ft.
Bedrooms: 3
Bathrooms: 3 ½
Width: 107' - 0"
Depth: 43' - 0"
Foundation: Unfinished
Walkout Basement
Price Code: C4

Order online @ eplans.com

PIGEON FALLS

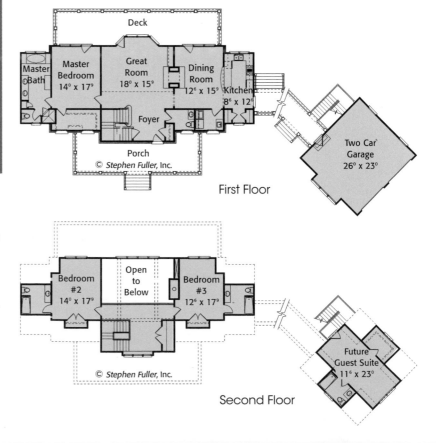

This expansive home is in harmony with its surroundings and in tune with the demands of today's lifestyles. Stonework and shingles echo wilderness textures and colors, yet the balanced roofline conveys a sense of tranquility. A wraparound porch is highly inviting. The foyer inside opens to the great room of elegant, soaring, two-story-high ceilings. A warming hearth links the great room and the dining room. There's plenty of opportunity for privacy in the master suite and upstairs bedrooms.

© Stephen Fuller, Inc.

SALEM FALLS

© Stephen Fuller, Inc.

Master Bedroom 19³ x 14⁰

Family Room 16⁶ x 18⁰

Breakfast 8⁹ x 10⁰

Kitchen 11⁶ x 12³

Two Car Garage

Dining Room 13⁶ x 15⁶

First Floor

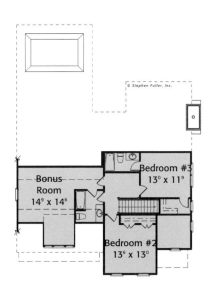

© Stephen Fuller, Inc.

Bonus Room 14⁹ x 14⁶

Bedroom #3 13⁰ x 11⁹

Bedroom #2 13⁶ x 13⁰

Second Floor

HPK3600023

First Floor: 1,872 sq. ft.
Second Floor: 643 sq. ft.
Total: 2,515 sq. ft.
Bonus Space: 328 sq. ft.
Bedrooms: 3
Bathrooms: 3 ½
Width: 46' - 0"
Depth: 66' - 0"
Foundation: Unfinished Basement
Price Code: C4

Order online @ eplans.com

This design offers Arts and Crafts style with porch details and an accent window. Inside, the formal dining room includes a tray ceiling. The family room is warmed by a massive hearth and accesses the rear porch. Secluded on the first floor, the master bedroom features a tray ceiling, porch access, a whirlpool tub, and His and Hers walk-in closets. Two additional bedrooms reside upstairs, along with a bonus room that easily converts to a fourth bedroom, home office, or playroom.

© Stephen Fuller, Inc.

HPK3600024

First Floor: 1,708 sq. ft.
Second Floor: 842 sq. ft.
Total: 2,550 sq. ft.
Bedrooms: 3
Bathrooms: 3 ½
Width: 107' - 0"
Depth: 51' - 0"
Foundation: Unfinished
Walkout Basement
Price Code: C4

Order online @ eplans.com

SILVER CREEK

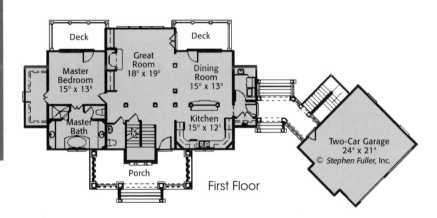

Deck

Deck

Master Bedroom
15⁰ x 13⁸

Great Room
18⁰ x 19⁰

Dining Room
15⁰ x 13⁴

Master Bath

Kitchen
15⁰ x 12⁵

Porch

Two-Car Garage
24⁴ x 21⁴
© Stephen Fuller, Inc.

First Floor

This plan is designed to gracefully complement a lake or mountain setting. The rooflines extend down to create porches for enjoying gentle breezes and spectacular views. Craftsman-style elements like board-and-batten siding and fieldstone facing enhance the connection with nature. Inside, a wide-open plan allows the great room, dining room, and kitchen to take advantage of beautiful views out the back. The master suite's private deck offers the homeowners a unique vantage point.

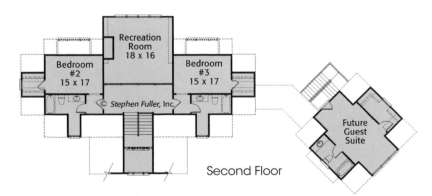

Recreation Room
18 x 16

Bedroom #2
15 x 17

Bedroom #3
15 x 17

© Stephen Fuller, Inc.

Future Guest Suite

Second Floor

VISALLA

HPK3600025

Square Footage: 2,598
Bedrooms: 3
Bathrooms: 2 ½
Width: 68' - 3"
Depth: 78' - 3"
Foundation: Finished
Walkout Basement
Price Code: C4

Order online @ eplans.com

The overall design of this home is reminiscent of a European country cottage. From the arched double-door entry, columns add a stately elegance to the foyer. A wall of French doors accesses the rear deck from the dining and great rooms. The formal dining room connects to the L-shaped kitchen. A box-bay breakfast nook opens to a wonderful keeping room. A large utility room separates two family bedrooms and their shared bath from the master suite. The bayed master bedroom suite features a beautiful coffered ceiling.

© Stephen Fuller, Inc.

HPK3600026

First Floor: 1,730 sq. ft.
Second Floor: 935 sq. ft.
Total: 2,665 sq. ft.
Bonus Space: 290 sq. ft.
Bedrooms: 4
Bathrooms: 4 ½
Width: 70' - 0"
Depth: 44' - 9"
Foundation: Crawlspace
Price Code: C4

Order online @ eplans.com

RIVER FALLS

First Floor

With plenty of space to gather both in-doors and out, this mountain-style lodge is a great place to escape from routine. Board and batten siding rises above a stone base, establishing the home as an outgrowth of its wilderness environment. Four bedrooms, each with its own bath, offer privacy to immediate and extended family. All are positioned to take advantage of rear views, and all have porch or deck access.

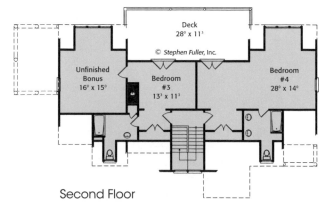

Second Floor

© Stephen Fuller, Inc.

ANNIVERSARY COTTAGE

Two Car Garage
23⁰ x 23⁰

© Stephen Fuller, Inc.

Deck

Kitchen
11⁰ x 11⁰

Great Room
20⁶ x 21⁶

Master Bedroom
18³ x 14³

Breakfast
15³ x 7⁹

Family Room
15³ x 9⁰

Dining Room
14⁹ x 13³

First Floor

Bedroom #2
13⁶ x 14³

Bedroom #3
12⁰ x 15⁶

Unfinished Bedroom
11³ x 15³

Study
8⁶ x 9⁰

Second Floor

HPK3600027

First Floor: 1,840 sq. ft.
Second Floor: 840 sq. ft.
Total: 2,680 sq. ft.
Bonus Space: 295 sq. ft.
Bedrooms: 3
Bathrooms: 2 ½
Width: 66' - 0"
Depth: 65' - 10"
Foundation: Crawlspace
Price Code: C4

Order online @ eplans.com

Multipane windows, shutters, and shingle accents adorn the stucco facade of this wonderful French Country home. Inside, the foyer introduces the hearth-warmed great room that features French-door access to the rear deck. The dining room, defined from the foyer and great room by columns, enjoys front-yard views. The master bedroom includes two walk-in closets, rear-deck access, and a dual vanity bath.

© Stephen Fuller, Inc.

HPK3600028

First Floor: 1,789 sq. ft.
Second Floor: 917 sq. ft.
Total: 2,706 sq. ft.
Bedrooms: 4
Bathrooms: 3 ½
Width: 51' - 6"
Depth: 65' - 0"
Foundation: Finished
Walkout Basement
Price Code: C4

Order online @ eplans.com

This plan opens with a striking octagonal dining room. A butler's pantry brings this room closer to the kitchen, making entertaining a breeze. For more casual meals, the bayed breakfast nook will be a favorite spot. A fireplace, built-in bookshelves, and back-deck views highlight the family room. The main floor finishes with a master suite that boasts a thoughtfully designed bath with separate vanities, a compartmented toilet, and a spa tub.

MAPLE STREET

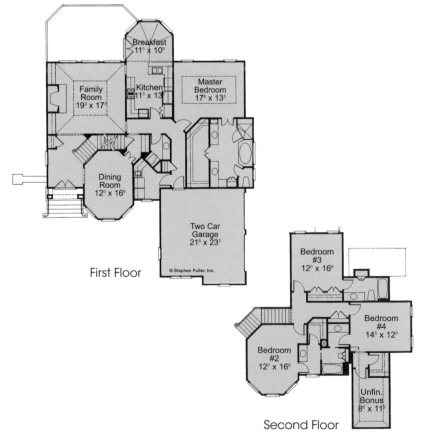

First Floor

© Stephen Fuller, Inc.

Breakfast
11³ x 10⁰

Family Room
19³ x 17³

Kitchen
11³ x 13

Master Bedroom
17⁶ x 13³

Dining Room
12⁰ x 16⁶

Two Car Garage
21⁹ x 23³

Second Floor

Bedroom #3
12⁰ x 16⁶

Bedroom #4
14⁰ x 12⁰

Bedroom #2
12⁰ x 16⁶

Unfin. Bonus
8⁶ x 11⁵

HOLLY RIDGE

First Floor

Second Floor

HPK3600029

First Floor: 1,650 sq. ft.
Second Floor: 1,060 sq. ft.
Total: 2,710 sq. ft.
Bedrooms: 4
Bathrooms: 3 ½
Width: 53' - 0"
Depth: 68' - 2"
Foundation: Finished
Walkout Basement
Price Code: C4

Order online @ eplans.com

This home, with its distinctive Georgian detailing, features keystone arches that frame the arched front door and windows. Inside, the foyer opens directly to the large great room with a fireplace. Adjacent to the breakfast room is the keeping room with a corner fireplace. The master suite contains dual vanities and a spacious walk-in closet. Upstairs, two family bedrooms enjoy separate access to a shared bath; a fourth bedroom offers a private bath.

©Stephen Fuller, Inc.

HPK3600030

First Floor: 1,763 sq. ft.
Second Floor: 947 sq. ft.
Total: 2,710 sq. ft.
Bedrooms: 3
Bathrooms: 2 ½
Width: 50' - 0"
Depth: 75' - 4"
Foundation: Unfinished Walkout Basement
Price Code: C4

Order online @ eplans.com

THOMASVILLE SHOWROOM

Superb French country design offers many special features. This classy home has a second-floor media room and adjoining exercise area. On the main level, a gourmet kitchen provides a snack counter and a walk-in pantry. A classic great room is warmed by a cozy fireplace and brightened by a wall of windows. An outdoor living area is spacious enough for grand events. Sweeping views and a fireplace in the master suite provide romance just for two.

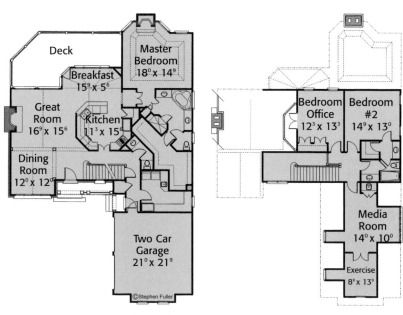

First Floor

Second Floor

©Stephen Fuller

ROD DENT 95

IVY GLEN

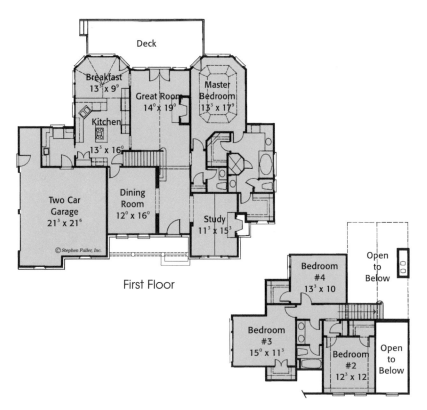

Deck

Breakfast
13³ x 9⁹

Great Room
14⁰ x 19⁰

Master
Bedroom
13³ x 17⁹

Kitchen
13³ x 16⁰

Two Car
Garage
21³ x 21⁶

Dining
Room
12⁰ x 16⁰

Study
11³ x 15³

©Stephen Fuller, Inc.

First Floor

Bedroom
#4
13³ x 10

Open
to
Below

Bedroom
#3
15⁰ x 11³

Bedroom
#2
12³ x 12

Open
to
Below

Second Floor

HPK3600031

First Floor: 1,932 sq. ft.
Second Floor: 807 sq. ft.
Total: 2,739 sq. ft.
Bedrooms: 4
Bathrooms: 2 ½
Width: 63' - 0"
Depth: 51' - 6"
Foundation: Finished
Walkout Basement
Price Code: C4

Order online @ eplans.com

This sensational country Colonial exterior is set off by a cozy covered porch. A two-story foyer opens to a quiet study with a centered fireplace. The gourmet kitchen features an island cooktop counter and a charming bayed breakfast nook. The great room soars two stories high but is made cozy with an extended-hearth fireplace. Two walk-in closets, a garden tub, and a separate shower highlight the master bath; a coffered ceiling decorates the master bedroom. Three family bedrooms, each with a walk-in closet, share a full bath upstairs.

HPK3600032

First Floor: 1,932 sq. ft.
Second Floor: 807 sq. ft.
Total: 2,739 sq. ft.
Bedrooms: 4
Bathrooms: 2 ½
Width: 63' - 0"
Depth: 51' - 6"
Foundation: Finished
Walkout Basement
Price Code: C4

Order online @ eplans.com

CHANTERELLE GLEN

First Floor

To the left of the recessed entry foyer, the box-windowed formal dining room leads to a large L-shaped kitchen with a separate utility area, an island cooktop, and a sunny bayed breakfast nook with deck access. The great room features a fireplace and rear access through French doors. The lavish master suite includes a bay-windowed sitting area. Two of the three second-floor bedrooms include walk-in closets.

Second Floor

© Stephen Fuller, Inc.

SILVER SPRINGS

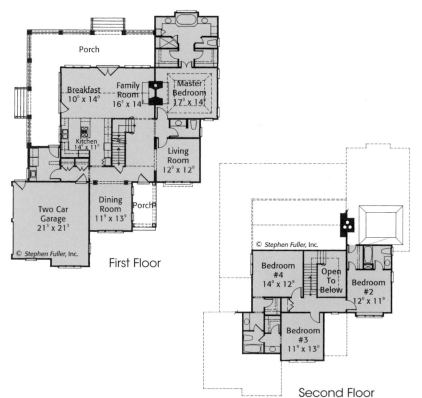

Porch

Breakfast
10⁰ x 14⁰

Family
Room
16⁰ x 14⁰

Master
Bedroom
17³ x 14⁰

Kitchen
14⁰ x 11⁰

Living
Room
12⁰ x 12⁰

Two Car
Garage
21³ x 21³

Dining
Room
11⁹ x 13⁹

Porch

© Stephen Fuller, Inc.

First Floor

© Stephen Fuller, Inc.

Bedroom
#4
14⁰ x 12⁹

Open
To
Below

Bedroom
#2
12⁰ x 11⁹

Bedroom
#3
11⁹ x 13⁰

Second Floor

An asymmetrical facade and a combination of rustic materials lend this design the cozy aspect of an old country home that has grown along with its family. Inside, a wide entry hall gives way to the formal living and dining rooms. Beyond the stairway lie the family gathering rooms and the kitchen, all of which are surrounded by a wide covered porch.

HPK3600034

First Floor: 1,900 sq. ft.
Second Floor: 890 sq. ft.
Total: 2,790 sq. ft.
Bedrooms: 4
Bathrooms: 2 ½
Width: 63' - 0"
Depth: 51' - 0"
Foundation: Finished
Walkout Basement
Price Code: C4

Order online @ eplans.com

CHESTNUT LANE

A perfect blend of stucco and stacked stone sets off keystones, transoms, and arches in this French Country facade to inspire an elegant spirit. The foyer is flanked by the spacious dining room and the study, which is accented by a vaulted ceiling and a fireplace. A great room with a full wall of glass connects the interior with the outdoors. A first-floor master suite offers both style and intimacy with a coffered ceiling and a secluded bath.

First Floor

Second Floor

© Stephen Fuller, Inc.

ARBORSHADE

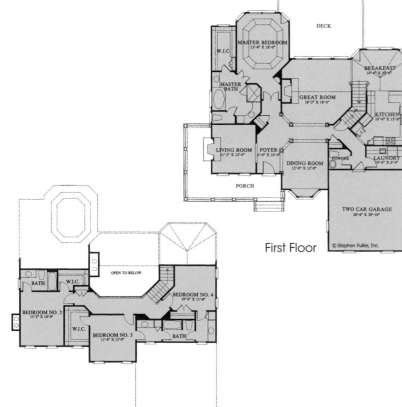

First Floor

© Stephen Fuller, Inc.

Second Floor

HPK3600035

First Floor: 1,840 sq. ft.
Second Floor: 950 sq. ft.
Total: 2,790 sq. ft.
Bedrooms: 4
Bathrooms: 3 ½
Width: 58' - 6"
Depth: 62' - 0"
Foundation: Finished
Walkout Basement
Price Code: C4

Order online @ eplans.com

The appearance of this Early-American home brings the past to mind with its wraparound porch and flower-box detailing. Columns frame the great room and dining room, while the living room enjoys a warming fireplace. The kitchen joins a sunny breakfast nook. A lavish master suite resides in privacy on the first floor, while three family bedrooms and two full baths make up the second floor.

HPK3600036

First Floor: 1,889 sq. ft.
Second Floor: 328 sq. ft.
Total: 2,217 sq. ft.
Bedrooms: 3
Bathrooms: 3
Width: 43' - 0"
Depth: 83' - 0"
Foundation: Slab
Price Code: C4

Order online @ eplans.com

Essentially a one-story, this country charmer houses the core of the home on the first level. Centered around the hearth-warmed great room, the layout is defined by spacious common areas and well-appointed sleeping quarters. The rear terrace is an added bonus.

CAMDEN

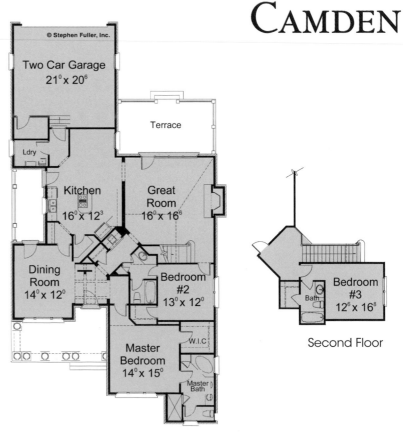

© Stephen Fuller, Inc.

Two Car Garage
21⁰ x 20⁶

Terrace

Ldry

Kitchen
16⁰ x 12³

Great Room
16⁰ x 16⁶

Dining Room
14⁰ x 12⁰

Bedroom #2
13⁰ x 12⁰

W.I.C

Master Bedroom
14⁰ x 15⁰

Master Bath

Bath

Bedroom #3
12⁶ x 16⁸

Second Floor

First Floor

© Stephen Fuller, Inc.

KESWICK

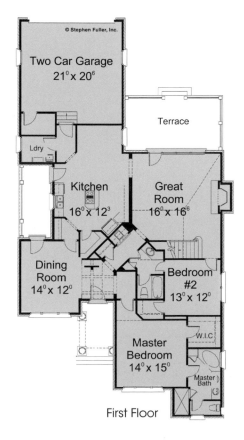

© Stephen Fuller, Inc.

Two Car Garage
21⁰ x 20⁶

Terrace

Ldry

Kitchen
16⁰ x 12³

Great
Room
16⁰ x 16⁶

Dining
Room
14⁰ x 12⁰

Bedroom
#2
13⁰ x 12⁰

W.I.C

Master
Bedroom
14⁰ x 15⁰

Master
Bath

First Floor

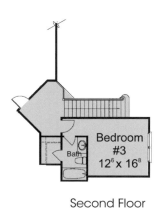

Bedroom
#3
12⁶ x 16⁸

Bath

Second Floor

HPK3600037

First Floor: 1,889 sq. ft.
Second Floor: 328 sq. ft.
Total: 2,217 sq. ft.
Bedrooms: 3
Bathrooms: 3
Width: 45' - 0"
Depth: 85' - 3"
Foundation: Crawlspace
Price Code: C4

Order online @ eplans.com

The exterior of this cottage is predominantly brick with accents of board and batten—double-hung windows and sidelights add to this cottage feel. Once inside, the foyer greets you with a cathedral ceiling; the master suite and a second bedroom are tucked away to the right. The spacious dining room is just on your left and has a French door leading to a side covered porch. The great room features a sloped ceiling that adds to the open feeling of this home. Upstairs you will find another bedroom and bath.

© Stephen Fuller, Inc.

HPK3600038

First Floor: 1,978 sq. ft.
Second Floor: 350 sq. ft.
Total: 2,328 sq. ft.
Bedrooms: 4
Bathrooms: 3 ½
Width: 57' - 3"
Depth: 65' - 0"
Foundation: Unfinished
Walkout Basement
Price Code: C4

Order online @ eplans.com

KENT PARK

First Floor

Second Floor

This design offers comfortable family living and an exterior that is influenced by early New England homes. Stone and siding, shutters, and flower boxes accent the Colonial lines. Inside, the artfully designed floor plan meets the needs of modern lifestyles. The family room includes a vaulted ceiling and a fireplace flanked by bookshelves. The kitchen and light-filled breakfast area form the heart of the downstairs plan. The master suite, set apart from the main rooms of the house, features a tray ceiling and sitting area.

© Stephen Fuller, Inc.

BARKSDALE

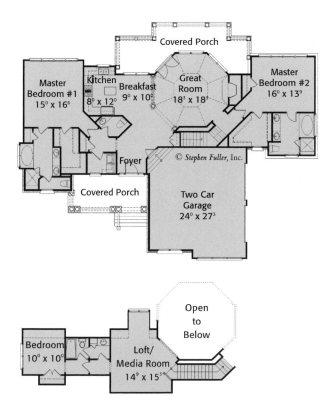

Covered Porch

Master
Bedroom #1
15⁰ x 16⁶

Kitchen
8⁰ x 12⁰

Breakfast
9⁰ x 10⁰

Great
Room
18³ x 18³

Master
Bedroom #2
16⁰ x 13⁹

Foyer

© Stephen Fuller, Inc.

Covered Porch

Two Car
Garage
24⁰ x 27³

Open
to
Below

Bedroom
10⁰ x 10⁰

Loft/
Media Room
14⁹ x 15³

HPK3600039

Square Footage: 2,457
Bedrooms: 2
Bathrooms: 2 ½
Width: 74' - 9"
Depth: 58' - 9"
Foundation: Crawlspace
Price Code: C4

Order online @ eplans.com

The striking plan makes a grand statement about honest materials, the value of crafts-manship, and luxurious livability. Double-gable styling adds interest to the roofline, while box bays add contrast below. Inside, the foyer leads to an octagonal great room with fireplace. A generous bay window/door configuration highlights this two-story-tall space and extends to the living space out-doors. Conveniently located on this floor are two master suites with spacious walk-in closets. Upstairs is an additional bedroom and a shared bath.

© Stephen Fuller, Inc.

HPK3600040

First Floor: 2,031 sq. ft.
Second Floor: 725 sq. ft.
Total: 2,756 sq. ft.
Bedrooms: 4
Bathrooms: 4 ½
Width: 81' - 0"
Depth: 45' - 0"
Foundation: Crawlspace
Price Code: C4

Order online @ eplans.com

CLOVERDALE

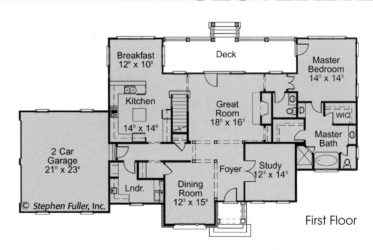

First Floor

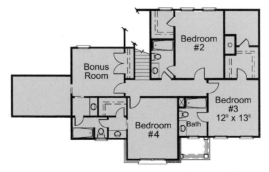

Second Floor

A careful combination of building materials—native stone and cedar shingles—gives warmth and architectural character to this home. The double porch adds a Charlestonian and southern feel to the home. Inside the formal dining room and study flank the foyer. A fireplace enhances the great room, making it the perfect place for casual gatherings. An island kitchen with the double sink overlooks the breakfast area. Upstairs you will find three bedrooms with spacious walk-in closets and a bonus room.

© Stephen Fuller, Inc.

BRISBOIS COURT

© Stephen Fuller, Inc.

HPK3600041

Square Footage: 1,684
Bedrooms: 3
Bathrooms: 2 ½
Width: 55' - 6"
Depth: 57' - 6"
Foundation: Finished
Walkout Basement
Price Code: C4

Order online @ eplans.com

Charming and compact, this one-story home is as beautiful as it is practical. The impressive arch over the double front door is repeated with an arched window in the formal dining room. This room opens to a spacious great room with fireplace and is near the kitchen and bayed breakfast area. Split sleeping arrangements put the master suite with His and Hers walk-in closets at the right of the plan and two family bedrooms at the left.

© Stephen Fuller, Inc.

HPK3600042

First Floor: 780 sq. ft.
Second Floor: 915 sq. ft.
Total: 1,695 sq. ft.
Bedrooms: 3
Bathrooms: 2 ½
Width: 41' - 0"
Depth: 41' - 0"
Foundation: Finished
Walkout Basement
Price Code: C4

Order online @ eplans.com

WINDERMERE COTTAGE

Columns, brickwork, and uniquely shaped windows and shutters remind us of the best homes of turn-of-the-century America. The large fireplace, framed by windows, creates a lovely focal point in the great room. Upstairs, double doors lead to the lavish master suite, which features a tray ceiling. Bedrooms 2 and 3 complete this floor, with a shared bath featuring private entrances.

First Floor

Second Floor

© Stephen Fuller, Inc.

ELLSWORTH MANOR

DECK

BREAKFAST
11'-4" X 8'-6"

BEDROOM NO. 3
11'-6" X 11'-0"

GREAT ROOM
14'-0" X 17'-6"

KITCHEN
11'-4" X 10'-0"

MASTER BEDROOM
12'-4" X 15'-6"

BATH

DN

HIS

FOYER
6'-6" X 6'-6"

PWDR.

MASTER BATH

BEDROOM NO. 2
11'-0" X 14'-8"

DINING ROOM
11'-4" X 10'-6"

LAUNDRY

HERS

TWO-CAR GARAGE
20'-4" X 19'-4"

©Stephen Fuller

HPK3600043

Square Footage: 1,733
Bedrooms: 3
Bathrooms: 2 ½
Width: 55' - 6"
Depth: 57' - 6"
Foundation: Finished Walkout Basement
Price Code: C4

Order online @ eplans.com

Delightfully different, this brick one-story home offers everything for the active family. The foyer opens to a formal dining room, accented with four columns, and a great room with a fireplace and French doors to the rear deck. The master suite features a tray ceiling, His and Hers walk-in closets, a double vanity, and a garden tub.

© Stephen Fuller, Inc.

HPK3600044

Square Footage: 1,770
Bedrooms: 3
Bathrooms: 2 ½
Width: 48' - 0"
Depth: 47' - 0"
Foundation: Finished
Walkout Basement
Price Code: L1

Order online @ eplans.com

HUNTINGTON WAY

Gables and a multilevel roof create the soft charm of this design. The foyer provides views into both the great room with a warming hearth and the dining room with a vaulted ceiling. The kitchen offers a spacious work area and opens to the adjacent breakfast room. Enter the master suite through large double doors and behold a tray ceiling and French doors leading to a private deck.

© Stephen Fuller, Inc.

HPK3600045

First Floor: 945 sq. ft.
Second Floor: 825 sq. ft.
Total: 1,770 sq. ft.
Bonus Space: 198 sq. ft.
Bedrooms: 3
Bathrooms: 2 ½
Width: 44' - 0"
Depth: 41' - 4"
Foundation: Unfinished Basement
Price Code: C4

Order online @ eplans.com

ADDISON

First Floor

Second Floor

Shutters, window boxes, and a square-columned porch add classic finishing touches to this design. The spacious great room, just past the ample foyer, features a fireplace flanked by built-in shelving and an angled border along the casual eating area. Upstairs, you'll find sleeping quarters plus a spacious study with a dormer. The generous master suite includes a walk-in closet and a large bath with separate tub, shower, and toilet compartments.

© Stephen Fuller, Inc.

HPK3600046

First Floor: 1,225 sq. ft.
Second Floor: 565 sq. ft.
Total: 1,790 sq. ft.
Bonus Space: 189 sq. ft.
Bedrooms: 3
Bathrooms: 2 ½
Width: 42' - 0"
Depth: 49' - 0"
Foundation: Finished
Walkout Basement
Price Code: C4

Order online @ eplans.com

CONCORD

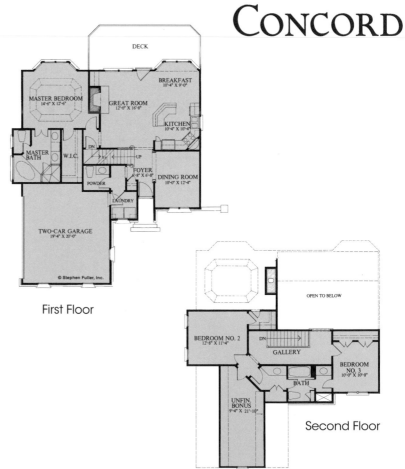

First Floor

Second Floor

This lovely home with mixed exterior materials is hard to beat. Both casual and formal occasions are accommodated from the great room with a fireplace to the formal dining room with front window views. An informal breakfast room complements the gourmet kitchen; its bay window makes family dining a treat. The first-floor master suite features a huge walk-in closet, corner tub, separate shower, and compartmented toilet. There are two family bedrooms upstairs.

© Stephen Fuller, Inc.

LINTON PARK

© Stephen Fuller, Inc.

HPK3600047

Square Footage: 1,800
Bedrooms: 3
Bathrooms: 2 ½
Width: 56' - 6"
Depth: 54' - 0"
Foundation: Unfinished
Walkout Basement
Price Code: C4

Order online @ eplans.com

This European-inspired cottage contains one of the most efficient floor plans available. From the formal dining room to the commodious great room, it accommodates various lifestyles in less than 2,000 square feet. An opulent master suite with deck access and a grand bath dominates the right wing. Two family bedrooms and a full bath are found to the left. The gourmet-style kitchen has an attached breakfast area with a glass bay for sunny brunches. An unfinished basement allows for future development.

© Stephen Fuller, Inc.

HPK3600048

Square Footage: 1,815
Bedrooms: 3
Bathrooms: 2 ½
Width: 60' - 0"
Depth: 58' - 6"
Foundation: Finished
Walkout Basement
Price Code: C4

Order online @ eplans.com

LYNDHURST LODGE

PORCH

BREAKFAST
10'-0" X 10'-0"

GREAT ROOM
16'-0" X 18'-0"

MASTER BEDROOM
15'-0" X 14'-0"

W.I.C.

MASTER BATH

POWDER

KITCHEN
14'-0" X 11'-4"

FOYER
5'-0" X 9'-0"

DINING ROOM
10'-6" X 13'-0"

BEDROOM
NO. 3
10'-6" X 10'-0"

BEDROOM NO. 2
11'-2" X 11'-0"

BATH

LAUND
5'-2" X
10'-6"

TWO CAR GARAGE
20'-4" X 19'-4"

© Stephen Fuller, Inc.

Inside, the foyer of this lovely European home opens into the great room with a vaulted ceiling and a dining room defined by columns. Cooking tasks are made easy with this home's step-saving kitchen and breakfast bar. Nestled away at the opposite end of the home, the master suite combines perfect solitude with elegant luxury. Features include a double-door entry, tray ceiling, and niche details. Two family bedrooms share a private bath.

TILLMAN

PORCH

BREAKFAST
10'-0" X 10'-0"

GREAT ROOM
16'-0" X 18'-0"

MASTER BEDROOM
15'-0" X 14'-0"

W.I.C.

MASTER BATH

POWDER

KITCHEN
14'-0" X 11'-4"

FOYER
5'-0" X 9'-0"

DINING ROOM
10'-6" X 13'-0"

BEDROOM NO. 2
11'-2" X 11'-0"

BEDROOM
NO. 3
10'-6" X 10'-0"

LAUND
5'-2" X
10'-6"

BATH

DN

TWO CAR GARAGE
20'-4" X 19'-4"

© Stephen Fuller, Inc.

HPK3600049

Square Footage: 1,815
Bedrooms: 3
Bathrooms: 2 ½
Width: 60' - 0"
Depth: 60' - 6"
Foundation: Finished
Walkout Basement
Price Code: C4

Order online @ eplans.com

With zoned living at the core of this floor plan, livability takes a convenient turn. The formal dining room is open to the central hallway and foyer, defined by columned archways. The great room has angled corners and a magnificent central fireplace and offers ample views to the rear grounds. Steps away is a well-lit breakfast room and a U-shaped kitchen with wrapping counter space. Two bedrooms share a full bath. The master suite includes a bath with a garden tub and a walk-in closet.

© Stephen Fuller, Inc.

HPK3600050

Square Footage: 1,850
Bedrooms: 3
Bathrooms: 2 ½
Width: 54' - 8"
Depth: 52' - 8"
Foundation: Finished
Walkout Basement
Price Code: C4

Order online @ eplans.com

YORKTOWN

This stately brick one-story home features a side-loading garage, which helps to maintain a beautiful facade. The elegant entry leads to a central hallway, connecting living areas and sleeping quarters, and opens to a formal dining room on the left. A splendid master suite with a coffered ceiling offers private access to the rear deck as well as a pleasant bath with a garden tub, glass-enclosed shower, and walk-in closet.

© Stephen Fuller, Inc.

© Stephen Fuller, Inc.

CAPE CHARLES PLACE

First Floor

Second Floor

HPK3600051

First Floor: 1,341 sq. ft.
Second Floor: 598 sq. ft.
Total: 1,939 sq. ft.
Bedrooms: 3
Bathrooms: 2
Width: 50' - 3"
Depth: 46' - 3"
Foundation: Crawlspace
Price Code: C4

Order online @ eplans.com

Horizontal siding, plentiful windows, and a wraparound porch grace this comfortable home. The great room is aptly named, with a fireplace, built-in seating, and access to the rear deck. Meal preparation is a breeze with an efficient galley kitchen; then dine on the screened porch. The first floor contains two bedrooms and a unique bath to serve family and guests. The second floor offers a private getaway with a master suite that supplies panoramic views from its adjoining sitting area.

© Stephen Fuller, Inc.

HPK3600052

Square Footage: 2,019
Bonus Space: 368 sq. ft.
Bedrooms: 3
Bathrooms: 2
Width: 56' - 0"
Depth: 56' - 3"
Foundation: Crawlspace
Price Code: C4

Order online @ eplans.com

WHITEFISH CANYON

This design takes inspiration from the casual fishing cabins of the Pacific Northwest and interprets it for modern livability. It offers three options for a main entrance. One door opens to a mud porch, while two French doors on the side porch open into a dining room with bay-window seating. Another porch entrance opens directly into the great room. The secluded master bedroom features a bath with a clawfoot tub and twin pedestal sinks. Two more bedrooms share a bath.

Copyright 1992 Stephen S. Fuller, Inc.

COLBURN COLONIAL

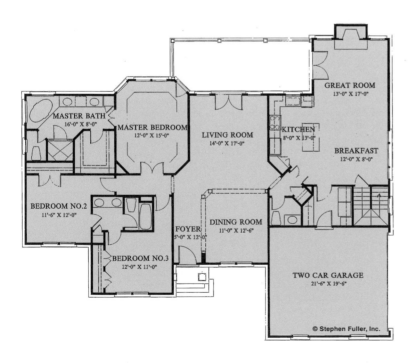

MASTER BATH
16'-0" X 8'-0"

MASTER BEDROOM
12'-0" X 15'-0"

LIVING ROOM
14'-0" X 17'-0"

GREAT ROOM
13'-0" X 17'-0"

KITCHEN
8'-0" X 13'-0"

BREAKFAST
12'-0" X 8'-0"

BEDROOM NO.2
11'-6" X 12'-0"

FOYER
5'-0" X 12'-0"

DINING ROOM
11'-0" X 12'-6"

BEDROOM NO.3
12'-0" X 11'-0"

TWO CAR GARAGE
21'-6" X 19'-6"

© Stephen Fuller, Inc.

HPK3600053

Square Footage: 2,077
Bedrooms: 3
Bathrooms: 2 ½
Width: 66' - 10"
Depth: 54' - 0"
Foundation: Finished
Walkout Basement
Price Code: C4

Order online @ eplans.com

A columned porch covers the entry to this single-story classic. The foyer opens to a living room full of windows and French doors to the rear deck. To the right, the spacious kitchen with a work island opens to a sunlit breakfast area and a great room that features a warming hearth and deck access. The master bath accommodates every need with His and Hers vanities, a garden tub, and walk-in closet. Two additional bedrooms share a compartmented bath.

© Stephen Fuller, Inc.

HPK3600054

Square Footage: 2,077
Bedrooms: 3
Bathrooms: 2 ½
Width: 66' - 0"
Depth: 54' - 0"
Foundation: Finished
Walkout Basement
Price Code: C4

Order online @ eplans.com

VAUGHN HOMESTEAD

European accents make this home a favorite. The foyer leads to the living room, which opens through French doors to the back property and to a banquet-sized dining room through a splendid colonnade. The spacious kitchen has a work island and a sunlit breakfast area that shares the warmth of a hearth from the great room. French doors open to the master suite, which features a lovely bay window and a lavish bath.

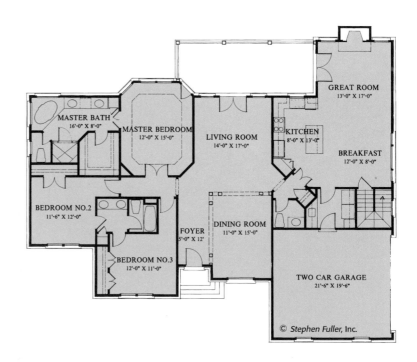

MASTER BATH
16'-0" X 8'-0"

MASTER BEDROOM
12'-0" X 15'-0"

LIVING ROOM
14'-0" X 17'-0"

GREAT ROOM
13'-0" X 17'-0"

KITCHEN
8'-0" X 13'-0"

BREAKFAST
12'-0" X 8'-0"

BEDROOM NO.2
11'-6" X 12'-0"

FOYER
5'-0" X 12'

DINING ROOM
11'-0" X 15'-0"

BEDROOM NO.3
12'-0" X 11'-0"

TWO CAR GARAGE
21'-6" X 19'-6"

© Stephen Fuller, Inc.

Jefferson Country

HPK3600055

Square Footage: 2,090
Bedrooms: 4
Bathrooms: 3
Width: 61' - 0"
Depth: 72' - 6"
Foundation: Unfinished
Walkout Basement
Price Code: C4

Order online @ eplans.com

Grace and elegance abound in this traditional, one-story, English country home. It contains all the necessary elements of a convenient floor plan as well: great room with fireplace, formal dining room, kitchen with attached breakfast nook, guest room/office, and three bedrooms including a master suite. A large, finished basement area allows for future expansion.

© Stephen Fuller, Inc.

HPK3600056

Square Footage: 2,090
Bedrooms: 4
Bathrooms: 3
Width: 61' - 0"
Depth: 72' - 0"
Foundation: Finished
Walkout Basement
Price Code: C4

Order online @ eplans.com

CANTERBURY RETREAT

This home's European styling will work well in a variety of environments. When it comes down to the details, this plan has it all. Begin with the front door, which opens into the dining and great rooms—the latter is complete with a fireplace and doors that open to the back porch. The kitchen combines with the breakfast nook to create ample space for meals. This plan incorporates four bedrooms; you may want to use one as an office and another as a study. The master bedroom houses a fabulous bath with twin walk-in closets and a spa tub.

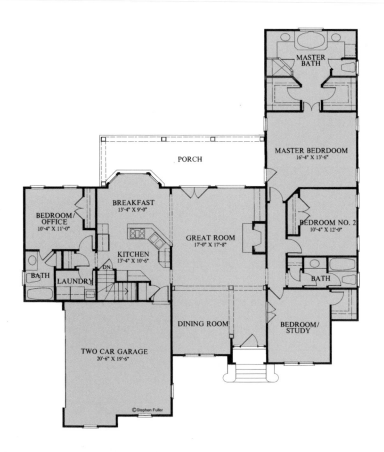

MASTER BATH

MASTER BEDRROOM
16'-4" X 13'-6"

PORCH

BREAKFAST
13'-4" X 9'-0"

BEDROOM/
OFFICE
10'-4" X 11'-0"

GREAT ROOM
17'-0" X 17'-8"

BEDROOM NO. 2
10'-4" X 12'-0"

KITCHEN
13'-4" X 10'-6"

BATH

LAUNDRY

DN.

BATH

TWO CAR GARAGE
20'-6" X 19'-6"

DINING ROOM

BEDROOM/
STUDY

©Stephen Fuller

© Stephen Fuller, Inc.

STANTON GABLE

First Floor

Second Floor

HPK3600057

First Floor: 1,053 sq. ft.
Second Floor: 1,053 sq. ft.
Total: 2,106 sq. ft.
Bonus Space: 212 sq. ft.
Bedrooms: 4
Bathrooms: 3
Width: 54' - 4"
Depth: 34' - 0"
Foundation: Finished
Walkout Basement
Price Code: C4

Order online @ eplans.com

Brick takes a bold stand in grand traditional style in this treasured design. The front study has a nearby full bath, making it a handy guest bedroom. The family room with a fireplace opens to a cozy breakfast area. The kitchen features a prep island and huge pantry. Upstairs, the master bedroom has its own sitting room and a giant closet. Two family bedrooms share a bath.

© Stephen Fuller, Inc.

HPK3600058

Square Footage: 2,120
Bedrooms: 3
Bathrooms: 3
Width: 62' - 0"
Depth: 62' - 6"
Foundation: Finished
Walkout Basement
Price Code: C4

Order online @ eplans.com

Stonemason Place

As quaint as the European countryside, this charming cottage boasts a unique interior. Living patterns revolve around the central family room—notice the placement of the formal dining room, kitchen with attached breakfast nook, and sunroom. Family bedrooms are tucked quietly away to the rear, while the master suite maintains privacy at the opposite end of the plan. A den with fireplace attaches to the master bedroom or can be accessed from the entry foyer. Bonus space in the basement can be developed later.

© Stephen Fuller

Tapping Reeve Retreat

Arched lintels and fanlight windows act as graceful accents for this design. The formal dining room is to the front of the plan and is open to the entry foyer. A private den also opens off the foyer with double doors. Bedrooms are split, with the master suite to the right side of the design and family bedrooms to the left.

© Stephen Fuller, Inc.

© Stephen Fuller, Inc.

HPK3600060

Square Footage: 2,150
Bedrooms: 3
Bathrooms: 2 ½
Width: 64' - 0"
Depth: 60' - 4"
Foundation: Finished
Walkout Basement
Price Code: C4

Order online @ eplans.com

SYCAMORE WALK

This home draws its inspiration from both French and English country homes. The dining room is subtly defined by the use of columns and a large triple window. The kitchen, with its work island, adjoins the breakfast area and keeping room with a fireplace. The home is completed by a master suite with a bay window and a garden tub. Space on the lower level can be developed later.

© Stephen Fuller, Inc.

WOODSIDE WALK

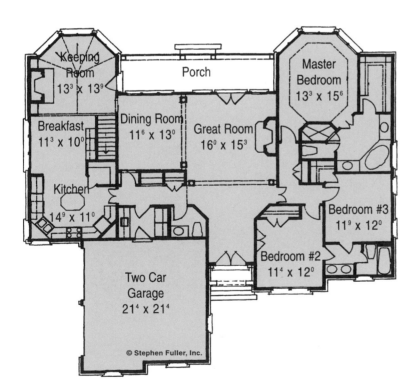

Keeping Room
13³ x 13⁹

Porch

Master Bedroom
13³ x 15⁶

Breakfast
11³ x 10⁰

Dining Room
11⁶ x 13⁰

Great Room
16⁰ x 15³

Kitchen
14⁹ x 11⁰

Bedroom #3
11⁹ x 12⁰

Two Car Garage
21⁴ x 21⁴

Bedroom #2
11⁴ x 12⁰

© Stephen Fuller, Inc.

HPK3600061

Square Footage: 2,150
Bedrooms: 3
Bathrooms: 2 ½
Width: 64' - 0"
Depth: 64' - 3"
Foundation: Finished Walkout Basement
Price Code: C4

Order online @ eplans.com

A recessed entry creates a warm welcome, while the Jack-arch window detailing adds intrigue to this charming exterior. The foyer, dining room, and great room are brought together in an open interior arrangement that's casually defined by decorative columns. The abundance of windows throughout the back of the home provides a grand view of the rear property. The master suite enjoys a garden tub, a large walk-in closet, and two vanities, for a perfect homeowner's retreat.

© Stephen Fuller, Inc.

HPK3600062

Square Footage: 2,170
Bedrooms: 4
Bathrooms: 3
Width: 62' - 0"
Depth: 61' - 6"
Foundation: Finished
Walkout Basement
Price Code: C4

Order online @ eplans.com

TYBEE

This classic cottage boasts a stone-and-wood exterior with a welcoming arch-top entry. An extended-hearth fireplace is the focal point of the family room, and a nearby sunroom opens up the living area to the outdoors. Sleeping quarters include a master wing with a spacious, angled bath and a sitting room or den that has its own full bath. On the opposite side of the plan, two family bedrooms share a full bath.

BEDROOM NO. 3
11'-6" X 11'-0"

BATH

MASTER BATH

W.I.C.

BEDROOM NO. 2
11'-4" X 11'-0"

SUN ROOM
12'-0" X 13'-8"

PORCH

MASTER BEDROOM
13'-4" X 15'-6"

PORCH

BREAKFAST
10'-0" X 9'-0"

FAMILY ROOM
18'-0" X 14'-0"

BATH

LAUNDRY

KITCHEN
12'-0" X 13'-2"

STORAGE

DN

DINING ROOM
11'-4" X 11'-4"

FOYER
6'-8" X 11'-10"

DEN/GUEST BEDROOM
11'-4" X 14'-0"

TWO CAR GARAGE
20'-4" X 19'-8"

PORCH

©Stephen Fuller

214 DOGWOOD WAY

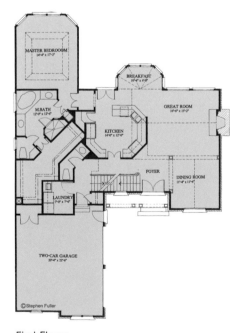

First Floor

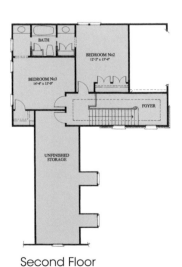

Second Floor

HPK3600063

First Floor: 1,580 sq. ft.
Second Floor: 595 sq. ft.
Total: 2,175 sq. ft.
Bedrooms: 3
Bathrooms: 2 ½
Width: 50' - 2"
Depth: 70' - 11"
Foundation: Finished
Walkout Basement
Price Code: C4

Order online @ eplans.com

Multipane windows and ink-black shutters stand out against the rich brick-and-clapboard backdrop. Inside, the spacious foyer leads directly to a large vaulted great room with its handsome fireplace. The dining room to the right of the foyer features a dramatic vaulted ceiling. In the privacy and quiet of the rear of the home is the master suite with its luxury bath and walk-in closet.

SWEETWOOD

A revisited farmhouse design shows style and smarts

ABOVE AND OPPOSITE: Prominent dormers and a nearly full-width front porch increase the home's curbside presence.

A standing-seam roof, dormer windows, and a side-gable exterior are prominent features of this updated farmhouse. Of course, the wide front porch adds the friendly, neighborhood touch that fans of the style enjoy. Note the alternate entry at the side of the plan, by way of the mudroom—a traditional detail that still makes sense for everyday family life.

The front of the home contains well-mannered formal spaces and thoughtful design touches. The foyer welcomes guests elegantly and introduces the dining room and living room, both of which afford attractive views of the forward property. The central stairway that leads to the second-floor landing does not look directly into upstairs bedrooms and baths, preserving privacy for family members.

At the rear of the plan is the family room, which continues through French doors onto the back deck. The room itself features a fireplace and matching built-in shelves, all perfectly proportioned for this largest of the home's spaces.

The kitchen and breakfast nook set the table for casual dining at the left of the plan, leaving room for a laundry room or pantry nearby. Bayed windows keep this hard-working part of the home well-lit.

LEFT: A curved stairway gently leads from the foyer to the second floor.

BELOW: The dining room is the most formal space in the home.

© Stephen Fuller, Inc.

HPK3600064

First Floor: 2,210 sq. ft.
Second Floor: 1,070 sq. ft.
Total: 3,280 sq. ft.
Bedrooms: 4
Bathrooms: 3 ½
Width: 60' - 6"
Depth: 58' - 6"
Foundation: Finished Walkout Basement
Price Code: L1

Order online @ eplans.com

ABOVE: The master suite is more luxurious than one would expect in a home of this size.

At the other side of the home is the master suite, complete with a rear-facing garden tub and very large wardrobe. A tray ceiling treatment and well-defined area for the bed are touches of refinement for the homeowners. The spacious deck at the back of the home, also accessible from the family room, is suited for everyday use as well as for larger entertaining.

The three bedrooms on the second level comfortably share two full baths. Each bedroom comes with deep reach-in closets and individual views of the surrounding landscape.

First Floor

Second Floor

LEFT: The well-lit kitchen encourages casual meals and everyday interaction between family members.

BELOW: Built-in shelves and an attractive fireplace anchor the main seating area in the family room.

HPK3600065

First Floor: 2,012 sq. ft.
Second Floor: 1,254 sq. ft.
Total: 3,266 sq. ft.
Bedrooms: 4
Bathrooms: 3 ½
Width: 70' - 0"
Depth: 75' - 6"
Foundation: Unfinished Basement
Price Code: L1

Order online @ eplans.com

HEDGEWOOD HEIGHTS

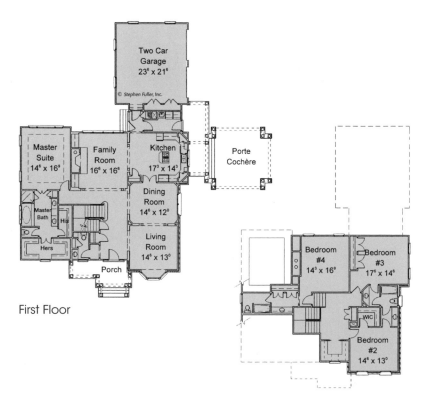

First Floor

Second Floor

Asymmetrical gables and a pedimented entry supported by double columns lend visual interest to this blended exterior. Inside, the wraparound hallway opens to the living and dining rooms and the family room. The gourmet kitchen easily serves the formal dining room and conveniently opens to the family room. The master suite is tucked into a private corner of the plan.

© Stephen Fuller, Inc.

BRIGHTON

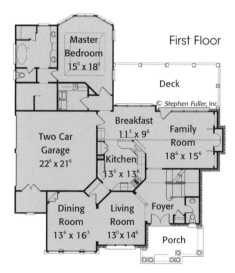

First Floor

Master Bedroom
15⁰ x 18⁰

Deck

© Stephen Fuller, Inc.

Two Car Garage
22⁶ x 21⁶

Breakfast
11³ x 9⁶

Kitchen
13⁰ x 13⁶

Family Room
18⁶ x 15⁶

Dining Room
13⁶ x 16³

Living Room
13⁰ x 14⁶

Foyer

Porch

HPK3600066

First Floor: 1,972 sq. ft.
Second Floor: 846 sq. ft.
Total: 2,818 sq. ft.
Bedrooms: 4
Bathrooms: 3 ½
Width: 57' - 3"
Depth: 65' - 0"
Foundation: Unfinished Walkout Basement
Price Code: C4

Order online @ eplans.com

Randomly stacked stone, artfully set against board-and-batten siding, offers a compelling focal point. Inside, the family room includes a vaulted ceiling and a fireplace flanked by bookshelves. The kitchen and breakfast area form the heart of the downstairs plan. The master suite, set apart from the public rooms, features a tray ceiling and comfortable sitting area. The upper floor offers three bedrooms and two baths. A loft provides a quiet study area or space for children to play.

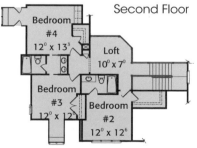

Second Floor

Bedroom #4
12⁰ x 13³

Loft
10⁰ x 7⁰

Bedroom #3
12⁰ x 12⁰

Bedroom #2
12⁰ x 12⁶

© Stephen Fuller, Inc.

HPK3600067

First Floor: 2,011 sq. ft.
Second Floor: 836 sq. ft.
Total: 2,847 sq. ft.
Bedrooms: 4
Bathrooms: 3 ½
Width: 58' - 3"
Depth: 66' - 3"
Foundation: Unfinished
Walkout Basement
Price Code: C4

Order online @ eplans.com

The exterior of this home exudes charm with arched, shuttered windows and sweeping gables. Inside, a column forms the living room entry, followed by the dining room. The circular kitchen and light-filled breakfast area are central to the downstairs plan. The thoughtfully secluded master suite, set apart from the main portion of the house in a separate wing, includes an amenity-filled bath and double walk-in closet. Three bedrooms, two baths, and a loft are upstairs.

St Charles

First Floor

Master Bedroom 15⁰ x 18⁰
Deck
© Stephen Fuller, Inc.
Two Car Garage 22⁰ x 21⁶
Breakfast 11⁶ x 11⁰
Great Room 18⁹ x 15⁶
Kitchen 13⁰ x 13⁶
Dining Room 13⁶ x 17⁶
Living Room 13⁰ x 14⁶
Foyer

Second Floor

Bedroom #4 12⁰ x 13⁰
Loft 11⁰ x 10⁶
Bedroom #3 12⁶ x 12⁰
Bedroom #2 12⁰ x 12⁰

© Stephen Fuller, Inc.

HPK3600068

First Floor: 1,795 sq. ft.
Second Floor: 1,068 sq. ft.
Total: 2,863 sq. ft.
Bonus Space: 344 sq. ft.
Bedrooms: 4
Bathrooms: 3 ½
Width: 78' - 9"
Depth: 49' - 9"
Foundation: Crawlspace
Price Code: C4

Order online @ eplans.com

Glen Oaks

First Floor

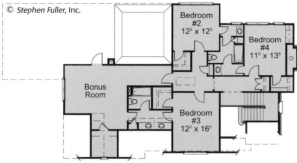

Second Floor

A distinctive center gable provides a focal point for this modern country exterior. Inside, the dining room features a bay window, and the great room offers built-in bookshelves and a wall of windows overlooking the rear deck. Sleeping areas consist of a private owner's suite and three second-floor bedrooms. A bonus room offers the possibility for expansion.

© Stephen Fuller, Inc.

HPK3600069

First Floor: 1,390 sq. ft.

Second Floor: 1,485 sq. ft.

Total: 2,875 sq. ft.

Bedrooms: 4

Bathrooms: 3 ½

Width: 52' - 9"

Depth: 43' - 0"

Foundation: Unfinished
Walkout Basement

Price Code: C4

Order online @ eplans.com

A side porch lends casual elegance to the exterior of this traditional home. The columned living room is directly off the foyer, then walk past the stairwell to a cozy family room with fireplace. The family room is open to the kitchen and breakfast nook. The formal dining room is accessible from the kitchen and is well appointed with a fireplace and access to the side porch. Living spaces are upstairs with a luxurious master suite, three additional bedrooms, and three baths.

COVINGTON COVE

First Floor

Second Floor

© Stephen Fuller, Inc.

BARNARD HEIGHTS

First Floor

Second Floor

HPK3600070

First Floor: 1,792 sq. ft.
Second Floor: 1,132 sq. ft.
Total: 2,924 sq. ft.
Bonus Space: 377 sq. ft.
Bedrooms: 4
Bathrooms: 3 ½
Width: 55' - 0"
Depth: 49' - 9"
Foundation: Crawlspace
Price Code: C4

Order online @ eplans.com

This appealing home features a box-bay window, flower boxes, and a front porch with a copper-seam roof. The front door flanked by transom windows opens to the dining room and great room. The great room provides a fireplace flanked by book-shelves and a set of French doors opening onto the rear deck. The breakfast room has direct access to the deck. A tray ceiling and a triple window highlight the master suite, which includes His and Hers walk-in closets. Upstairs houses three bedrooms, two full baths, and a large bonus room.

© Stephen Fuller, Inc.

HPK3600071

First Floor: 1,809 sq. ft.

Second Floor: 1,118 sq. ft.

Total: 2,927 sq. ft.

Bedrooms: 4

Bathrooms: 3 ½

Width: 55' - 0"

Depth: 51' - 0"

Foundation: Crawlspace

Price Code: C4

Order online @ eplans.com

EAST BENNINGTON PLACE

First Floor

The pedimented porch and paneled front door of this spacious home leads to a foyer that includes a coat closet and powder room. A comfortable floor plan boasts decorative columns that help define the foyer, dining room, and great room that opens to the back deck. The master suite, thoughtfully set apart from the family bedrooms, features double doors that open to a spacious bath with a garden tub and double vanities. The second floor offers three bedrooms and a bonus that could be a media room or a children's playroom.

Second Floor

© Stephen Fuller, Inc.

DELMONT

First Floor

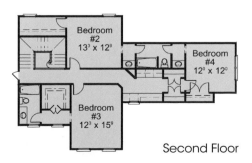

Second Floor

HPK3600072

First Floor: 1,845 sq. ft.
Second Floor: 1,092 sq. ft.
Total: 2,937 sq. ft.
Bedrooms: 4
Bathrooms: 3 ½
Width: 87' - 0"
Depth: 46' - 3"
Foundation: Crawlspace
Price Code: C4

Order online @ eplans.com

The appearance of this country style brings the past to mind with its wraparound porch, wood siding, and stone accents. Inside the foyer opens to the dining room on the right and leads to an architectural highlight of this home—the staircase which is centrally located. The great room just off to the left of the home features a fireplace a box-beamed ceiling. The kitchen features an island and a walk-in closet. Upstairs you will find three bedrooms and two bathrooms.

HPK3600073

First Floor: 1,845 sq. ft.
Second Floor: 1,092 sq. ft.
Total: 2,937 sq. ft.
Bedrooms: 4
Bathrooms: 3 ½
Width: 87' - 0"
Depth: 46' - 3"
Foundation: Crawlspace
Price Code: C4

Order online @ eplans.com

CLARENDON SPRINGS

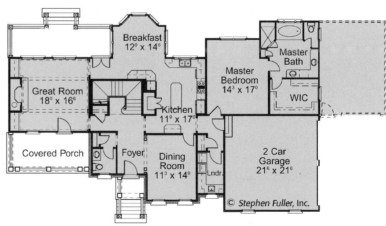

First Floor

The great room is the heart of this home. The foyer leads through a central vestibule to the grand living area, which has a fireplace framed by built-in bookshelves. The kitchen features a large island, walk-in pantry, and ample countertop and cabinet space. The master suite is secluded off the kitchen and is close to the laundry room. Upstairs Bedrooms 2 and 4 share a bathroom, while Bedroom 3 has its own private bathroom.

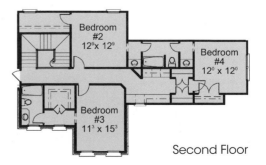

Second Floor

© Stephen Fuller, Inc.

WESTWOOD

© Stephen Fuller, Inc.

First Floor

Second Floor

HPK3600074

First Floor: 1,760 sq. ft.
Second Floor: 1,186 sq. ft.
Total: 2,946 sq. ft.
Bedrooms: 4
Bathrooms: 3 ½
Width: 78' - 9"
Depth: 42' - 0"
Foundation: Crawlspace
Price Code: C4

Order online @ eplans.com

This charming exterior conceals a perfect family plan with spaces designed for the way people live today. A kitchen filled with modern amenities features a door leading to the deck and a breakfast area with a triple window that draws in natural light. The master suite is tucked away for a private retreat. Upstairs you will find three bedrooms and a bonus room that could become a fifth bedroom if needed. Two of the bedrooms share a Jack-and-Jill bath while the third has its own private bath.

© Stephen Fuller, Inc.

HPK3600075

First Floor: 1,760 sq. ft.

Second Floor: 1,186 sq. ft.

Total: 2,946 sq. ft.

Bedrooms: 4

Bathrooms: 3 ½

Width: 78' - 9"

Depth: 49' - 0"

Foundation: Crawlspace

Price Code: C4

Order online @ eplans.com

DUNNINGTON

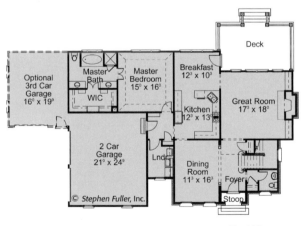

First Floor

This welcoming entrance combines a brick-and-siding facade with lintels, shutters, and gables. The facade conceals a floor plan that accommodates both large groups and small gatherings with ease. The L-shaped kitchen overlooks a bright breakfast area with triple window views and access to the rear deck. The great room features a cozy fireplace and built-in bookshelves. Upstairs, three bedrooms, two full baths, and a bonus room offer plenty of room for the family.

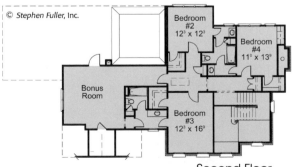

Second Floor

© Stephen Fuller, Inc.

HAINESPORT

First Floor

Second Floor

HPK3600076

First Floor: 1,849 sq. ft.
Second Floor: 1,098 sq. ft.
Total: 2,947 sq. ft.
Bedrooms: 4
Bathrooms: 3 ½
Width: 72' - 0"
Depth: 46' - 0"
Foundation: Crawlspace
Price Code: C4

Order online @ eplans.com

Casement windows topped by transoms, an elliptical window, and a double front door capture light and views. Exterior materials of brick and cedar shingles give the design the cozy look of a country retreat with a slight Cape Code feel. Once inside, an open floor plan undermines the home's informality. The kitchen features a walk-in pantry and a large work island. The great room accesses both porches. The first floor master suite is tucked away for ultimate privacy. The second floor holds three additional bedrooms and two baths.

© Stephen Fuller, Inc.

HPK3600077

First Floor: 1,809 sq. ft.
Second Floor: 1,148 sq. ft.
Total: 2,957 sq. ft.
Bedrooms: 4
Bathrooms: 3 ½
Width: 55' - 0"
Depth: 51' - 9"
Foundation: Crawlspace
Price Code: C4

Order online @ eplans.com

ARLINGTON HEIGHTS

First Floor

Second Floor

This two-story home reflects the Colonial architecture of the South, with a columned entry and paneled shutters. Inside decorative columns open the foyer to the formal dining room and great room. Planned events are easily handled with the butler's pantry off the kitchen. The master suite is tucked away off the kitchen for seclusion. Two upstairs bedrooms share a full bath while the other bedroom has a private bathroom. The second floor would not be complete without a large bonus room.

© Stephen Fuller, Inc.

CHANNING PLACE

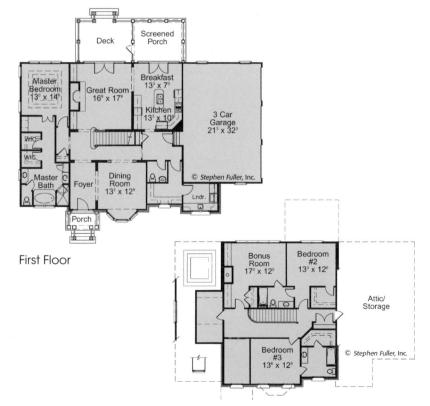

Deck | Screened Porch

Master Bedroom 13⁰ x 14⁰

Great Room 16⁹ x 17⁹

Breakfast 13³ x 7⁹

Kitchen 13³ x 10⁹

3 Car Garage 21³ x 32³

WIC

WIC

Master Bath | Foyer | Dining Room 13³ x 12⁹

Lndr.

Porch

© Stephen Fuller, Inc.

First Floor

Bonus Room 17⁰ x 12⁰

Bedroom #2 13³ x 12⁰

Attic/ Storage

Bedroom #3 13⁶ x 12⁰

© Stephen Fuller, Inc.

Second Floor

HPK3600078

First Floor: 1,856 sq. ft.
Second Floor: 1,144 sq. ft.
Total: 3,000 sq. ft.
Bedrooms: 3
Bathrooms: 3 ½
Width: 66' - 6"
Depth: 54' - 9"
Foundation: Crawlspace
Price Code: C4

Order online @ eplans.com

Classic in proportion and slightly Georgian in attitude, this home boasts a rich architectural heritage that traces back to early America. Just off the foyer, the formal dining room is enhanced by a lovely bay window and is defined by columns and cased openings. French doors open the great room onto the deck and the breakfast area onto a screened porch. The master suite features a tray ceiling while the bathroom offers a separate dressing area, His and Hers walk-in closets, double vanities, and a large shower.

© Stephen Fuller, Inc.

HPK3600079

First Floor: 1,856 sq. ft.
Second Floor: 1,144 sq. ft.
Total: 3,000 sq. ft.
Bedrooms: 3
Bathrooms: 3 ½
Width: 66' - 6"
Depth: 57' - 6"
Foundation: Crawlspace
Price Code: C4

Order online @ eplans.com

EAST HAMPTON

Windows featuring Jack-arch detailing and raised-panel shutters combine with brick and wood to create the timeless character of this home. The foyer leads to a spacious great room and a dining room. A useful feature: the office located just off the laundry room. The master bedroom and bath, complete with His and Hers vanities and walk-in closets, are privately located at the rear of the home. Upstairs, there are two additional bedrooms, which include spacious walk-in closets and private bathrooms.

© Stephen Fuller, Inc.

GUILFORD CORNERS

HPK3600080

First Floor: 1,886 sq. ft.
Second Floor: 1,162 sq. ft.
Total: 3,048 sq. ft.
Bedrooms: 3
Bathrooms: 3 ½
Width: 66' - 6"
Depth: 57' - 3"
Foundation: Crawlspace
Price Code: C4

Order online @ eplans.com

First Floor

Second Floor

The brick-and-shake exterior of this home is set off by a cozy, covered porch, perfect for enjoying cool evenings outside. The foyer opens to the dining room defined by double-hung windows and cased openings. Just beyond, the kitchen features an island cooktop counter and a breakfast nook leading to a screened porch. Two walk-in closets, a garden tub, and a separate shower highlight the master bath, while a tray ceiling decorates the master bedroom. Upstairs are two secondary bedrooms with their own private bathrooms and spacious walk-in closets.

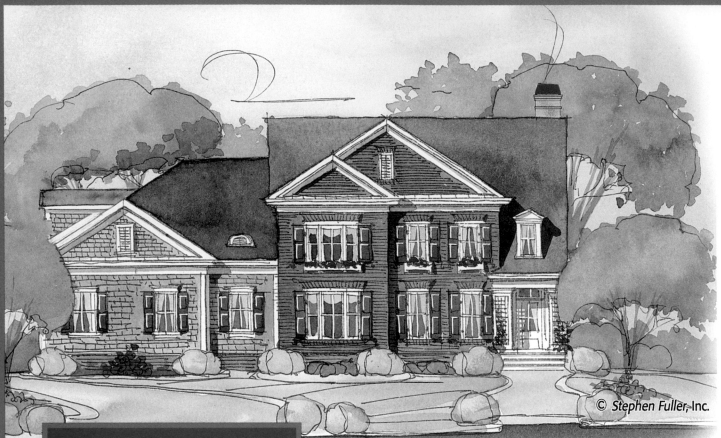

© Stephen Fuller, Inc.

HPK3600081

First Floor: 2,146 sq. ft.
Second Floor: 913 sq. ft.
Total: 3,059 sq. ft.
Bonus Space: 355 sq. ft.
Bedrooms: 3
Bathrooms: 3 ½
Width: 82' - 6"
Depth: 45' - 3"
Foundation: Crawlspace
Price Code: C4

Order online @ eplans.com

NEWBERRY HEIGHTS

First Floor

Nine-foot ceilings on the main level contribute to open, bright interiors. A wall creates definition between the formal dining and living rooms. The dining room leads back to a spacious kitchen with a large prep island. The great room features bookshelves flanking the fireplace and three large windows overlooking the deck. Upstairs, you will find two bedrooms with their own bathrooms as well as bonus room that could become a third bedroom if needed.

© Stephen Fuller, Inc.

Second Floor

© Stephen Fuller, Inc.

SUMMERVILLE

First Floor

Deck

Covered Porch

Breakfast/ Keeping 22⁰ x 16⁰

Master Bedroom 13³ x 20³

Kitchen 12³ x 12⁰

Great Room 17⁶ x 16³

Two Car Garage 22⁰ x 27⁶

Dining Room 16³ x 14⁰

Foyer

Bedroom #2 12⁰ x 11⁰

Bedroom #3 13⁶ x 12⁰

© Stephen Fuller, Inc.

Bedroom #4 12⁰ x 19⁰

© Stephen Fuller, Inc.

Second Floor

HPK3600082

First Floor: 2,735 sq. ft.
Second Floor: 375 sq. ft.
Total: 3,110 sq. ft.
Bedrooms: 4
Bathrooms: 3 ½
Width: 73' - 9"
Depth: 63' - 0"
Foundation: Unfinished Walkout Basement
Price Code: L1

Order online @ eplans.com

When looking for a design, this home offers all the features that today's clients are looking for. The spacious dining room is just off to the left of the foyer and features a butler's pantry and direct access to the kitchen. The kitchen features a serving bar and opens to the keeping room. The stone fireplace in the family room adds warmth and ambiance. All bedrooms are located in the right wing for complete privacy. The laundry is just off the master and near the other bedrooms.

HPK3600083

First Floor: 2,489 sq. ft.
Second Floor: 659 sq. ft.
Total: 3,148 sq. ft.
Bedrooms: 4
Bathrooms: 3 ½
Width: 71' - 9"
Depth: 56' - 9"
Foundation: Unfinished
Walkout Basement
Price Code: L1

Order online @ eplans.com

BRIAR VISTA

First Floor

© Stephen Fuller, Inc.

With a master bedroom, second bedroom, and study on the main level and stairs tucked away off the breakfast area, the layout of this versatile two-story house behaves like a ranch. Two upstairs bedrooms, a shared bath, and bonus space are perfect for guests or older children. They also free the downstairs bedroom for use as a private study or sitting room. A great room with a fireplace occupies the heart of the house. Two bays off the kitchen create an enticing sunroom and breakfast area.

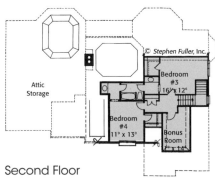

Second Floor

© Stephen Fuller, Inc.

HPK3600084

First Floor: 2,785 sq. ft.
Second Floor: 447 sq. ft.
Total: 3,232 sq. ft.
Bedrooms: 4
Bathrooms: 3 ½
Width: 75' - 0"
Depth: 63' - 0"
Foundation: Unfinished
Walkout Basement
Price Code: L1

Order online @ eplans.com

Winfield

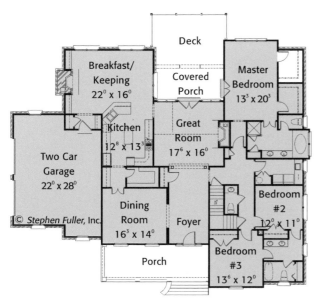

First Floor

Bedroom #4
16³ x 19⁰

© Stephen Fuller, Inc.

Second Floor

Stately and charming, this home embraces visitors with a pedimented entry and a front porch. Inside, the foyer leads to a cozy great room warmed by a fireplace and French doors to the rear covered porch. The kitchen boasts a center island and breakfast bar opening to the keeping/breakfast room. This room is flooded with light and features a sloped ceiling, fireplace, and built-in cabinetry. The master bedroom is dinstinguished by a tray ceiling. Two additional bedrooms each with private baths and walk-in closets.

HPK3600085

First Floor: 1,876 sq. ft.

Second Floor: 1,374 sq. ft.

Total: 3,250 sq. ft.

Bonus Space: 299 sq. ft.

Bedrooms: 4

Bathrooms: 3

Width: 62' - 3"

Depth: 44' - 3"

Foundation: Unfinished Walkout Basement

Price Code: L1

Order online @ eplans.com

AFTON VIEW

First Floor

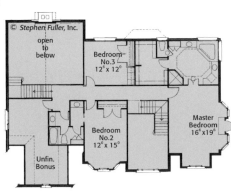

Second Floor

Large bays in the living room and master suite add excitement to this efficient floor plan. With the formal living and dining rooms to the right, and the kitchen, breakfast, and great room to the rear, it is an ideal home for entertaining. A large deck creates extra gathering space outdoors at an affordable price. The guest bedroom and full bath make it a great plan for accommodating out-of-town guests. Front and back staircases lead to the upper story, where a master suite provides perfect solitude.

© Stephen Fuller, Inc.

LEXINGTON HEIGHTS

First Floor

With its simple lines, this plan has a touch of Colonial and southern vernacular. The foyer leads to a spacious, two-story great room. The kitchen features a prep island, breakfast bar, and wet bar island opening to the great room. Both the great room and the breakfast area are surrounded by a wall of windows. The master suite is tucked away, just off the breakfast room. The master bath features a separate shower, garden tub, His and Hers vanities, and a separate dressing/make-up area.

Second Floor

© Stephen Fuller, Inc.

HPK3600087

First Floor: 2,198 sq. ft.
Second Floor: 1,133 sq. ft.
Total: 3,331 sq. ft.
Bedrooms: 4
Bathrooms: 3 ½
Width: 66' - 0"
Depth: 59' - 0"
Foundation: Crawlspace
Price Code: C4

Order online @ eplans.com

WINCHESTER

This home exudes traditional style with gables, stone, clapboard siding, and shuttered windows. Inside, classic and contemporary combine for a home that is welcoming to all. The dining room is located off of the foyer, which leads into a two-story great room featuring a fireplace and windows flanked by doors leading to the expansive rear deck. The kitchen and breakfast room are combined for family gatherings and the master suite occupies the entire left wing. Three bedrooms and two baths are located upstairs.

© Stephen Fuller, Inc.

First Floor

Second Floor

© Stephen Fuller, Inc.

COTSWOLD PLACE

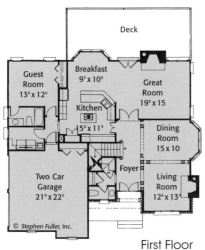

First Floor

Deck

Guest Room 13⁶ x 12⁰

Breakfast 9³ x 10⁰

Great Room 19⁹ x 15

Kitchen 15⁰ x 11⁹

Dining Room 15 x 10

Two Car Garage 21⁹ x 22³

Foyer

Living Room 12⁶ x 13⁹

© Stephen Fuller, Inc.

Bedroom #4 13⁶ x 13⁰

Master Bath

Master Bedroom 19⁹ x 15³

Bedroom #3 13⁶ x 12⁹

Study 12⁵ x 11³

© Stephen Fuller, Inc.

Second Floor

HPK3600088

First Floor: 1,678 sq. ft.
Second Floor: 1,677 sq. ft.
Total: 3,355 sq. ft.
Bedrooms: 4
Bathrooms: 3 ½
Width: 51' - 6"
Depth: 50' - 0"
Foundation: Unfinished Walkout Basement
Price Code: L1

Order online @ eplans.com

Stone accents and a covered porch recall the privacy of a country retreat. The U-shaped staircase creates interest without added cost. The foyer opens to a vaulted living room with a bay window. Double doors lead from the foyer to the family room/kitchen/breakfast area accented by a window wall and central fireplace. A guest suite is also on the main level. The second floor provides two additional bedrooms and a bath, plus a secluded master suite with a fireplace, private study, and luxurious bath.

© Stephen Fuller, Inc.

HPK3600089

First Floor: 2,023 sq. ft.
Second Floor: 1,337 sq. ft.
Total: 3,360 sq. ft.
Bedrooms: 4
Bathrooms: 3 ½
Width: 78' - 0"
Depth: 64' - 0"
Foundation: Crawlspace
Price Code: C4

Order online @ eplans.com

NORWALK

This early American home brings the past to mind with its wraparound porch and exterior materials. The two-story foyer opens to the dining room and leads back to the great room. The galley kitchen features a prep island and opens to the sun-filled breakfast room and great room. Stairs to the second level lead to three additional bedrooms with plenty of closet space and a variety of bath arrangements. A playroom with ample storage completes the upstairs level.

First Floor

Second Floor

WESSINGTON PLACE

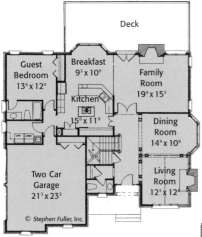

First Floor

Deck

Guest Bedroom
13⁶ x 12⁰

Breakfast
9³ x 10⁰

Family Room
19⁹ x 15³

Kitchen
15⁶ x 11⁹

Dining Room
14⁹ x 10⁹

Two Car Garage
21³ x 23³

Living Room
12³ x 12⁶

© Stephen Fuller, Inc.

Second Floor

Bedroom #4
13⁶ x 13⁰

Master Bedroom
19⁹ x 15³

© Stephen Fuller, Inc.

Study
12³ x 11³

Bedroom #3
13⁶ x 12³

HPK3600090

First Floor: 1,612 sq. ft.
Second Floor: 1,766 sq. ft.
Total: 3,378 sq. ft.
Bedrooms: 4
Bathrooms: 3 ½
Width: 52' - 0"
Depth: 50' - 6"
Foundation: Unfinished Walkout Basement
Price Code: L1

Order online @ eplans.com

A brick exterior with pedimented gables provides a traditional welcome. A compact plan allows this home to work on many narrow lots. The garage is set forward so it also works well on property that slopes front to back. Inside, the spacious master suite boasts its own study and allows great flexibility. The guest suite at the rear of the home offers great privacy. Bay windows in the living and breakfast rooms let in added light and create aesthetic interest without huge expense.

© Stephen Fuller, Inc.

HPK3600091

First Floor: 2,149 sq. ft.
Second Floor: 1,243 sq. ft.
Total: 3,392 sq. ft.
Bedrooms: 4
Bathrooms: 3 ½
Width: 74' - 9"
Depth: 55' - 0"
Foundation: Crawlspace
Price Code: C4

Order online @ eplans.com

SHELBURNE

Siding and stone combine to give this home cottage appeal. It features a three-car garage in a two-bay/single-bay combination. This allows the home's architectural appeal to remain the focus. The charming front porch wraps around the windows of the formal dining room. Inside, the foyer opens to the two-story great room. The galley-style kitchen features a working island and opens into the sunlit breakfast room. Upstairs, three family bedrooms and two full baths complement a flexible bonus room.

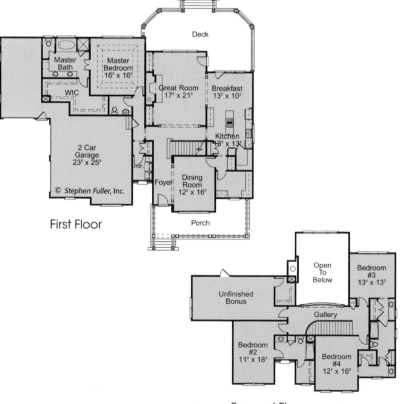

First Floor

Second Floor

© Stephen Fuller, Inc.

TRENTON PLACE

First Floor

Second Floor

HPK3600092

First Floor: 2,149 sq. ft.
Second Floor: 1,243 sq. ft.
Total: 3,392 sq. ft.
Bedrooms: 4
Bathrooms: 3 ½
Width: 74' - 0"
Depth: 51' - 0"
Foundation: Crawlspace
Price Code: C4

Order online @ eplans.com

Classic in proportion and Georgian in attitude, this home boasts a rich architectural heritage. It rearranges the usual symmetry of a Georgian plan in favor of the open configuration that works well for modern-day living. The family room offers a fireplace with built-ins, and an eat-in kitchen has a pantry and a butler's pantry that serves the dining room. A deck invites outdoor dining. Tucked away is the master suite, with a large walk-in closet. Upstairs are three additional bedrooms and a bonus room.

© Stephen Fuller, Inc.

HPK3600093

First Floor: 2,233 sq. ft.
Second Floor: 1,161 sq. ft.
Total: 3,394 sq. ft.
Bedrooms: 4
Bathrooms: 3 ½
Width: 66' - 0"
Depth: 52' - 3"
Foundation: Crawlspace
Price Code: C4

Order online @ eplans.com

PENDLETON PLACE

First Floor

Second Floor

This stately home features a side-loading garage, which helps maintain a beautiful facade. If needed, a single-bay garage can be added off the master suite. The elegant entry leads to a central hallway that opens to the formal dining room, followed by a two-story great room. Natural light and views of the backyard show off the great room, which includes a handsome fireplace and built-ins. A secluded first-floor master suite with a tray ceiling is complemented by three second-floor bedrooms and a bonus room.

© Stephen Fuller, Inc.

LENOX

© Stephen Fuller, Inc.

First Floor

Grilling Deck

Gathering Room
18⁰ x 14⁶

Summer Porch

Breakfast
10⁰ x 12⁰

Kitchen
20⁰ x 14⁰

Living Room
19⁰ x 15⁰

Master Bedroom
15⁹ x 17⁶

Dining Room
13⁰ x 15⁰

Porch

Two Car Garage
22⁰ x 23⁰

© Stephen Fuller, Inc.

Bedroom #3
12³ x 13³

Open To Below

Bedroom #4
13³ x 13⁹

Attic

Bedroom #2
13⁰ x 12⁹

Open To Below

Unfin. Bonus
9⁹ x 19⁹

Second Floor

HPK3600094

First Floor: 2,397 sq. ft.
Second Floor: 1,051 sq. ft.
Total: 3,448 sq. ft.
Bedrooms: 4
Bathrooms: 3 ½
Width: 72' - 3"
Depth: 66' - 0"
Foundation: Unfinished Walkout Basement
Price Code: L1

Order online @ eplans.com

This New American-style home is a warm mixture of both classic and casual styles. Traditional in spirit, the design was developed with careful attention to detail. The multigabled roofline, shuttered windows, and columned front porch are all inviting elements of the home. This home plan features an open, two-story foyer with a full-length window to welcome guests inside. At the heart of this plan lies the kitchen. The hallmark of this layout is an L-shaped island, a built-in desk, and ample storage and workspace.

© Stephen Fuller, Inc.

HPK3600095

First Floor: 2,314 sq. ft.
Second Floor: 1,177 sq. ft.
Total: 3,491 sq. ft.
Bedrooms: 4
Bathrooms: 3 ½
Width: 67' - 0"
Depth: 52' - 0"
Foundation: Unfinished
Walkout Basement
Price Code: L1

Order online @ eplans.com

GREENWOOD

First Floor

Simple elegance never goes out of style, as this home illustrates. Flower boxes and arched windows add graceful touches to this expansive home's brick exterior. Inside, a central great room facilitates family communication. A very workable floor plan includes a private rear office, a huge breakfast area, and a living room that can convert to a study for the master bedroom. Stairs are centrally located and economical to build. All three children's bedrooms are upstairs and have spacious walk-in closets.

Second Floor

© Stephen Fuller, Inc.

FINLEY HILL

HPK3600096

Square Footage: 2,800
Bedrooms: 3
Bathrooms: 2 ½
Width: 73' - 2"
Depth: 57' - 3"
Foundation: Unfinished
Walkout Basement
Price Code: C4

Order online @ eplans.com

This quaint cottage is reminiscent of homes built centuries ago. Interior details, such as the tray-ceilinged foyer and exposed beams in the kitchen, add luxury. Visitors are led from the foyer to a study, or straight ahead to the great room with French doors to the porch that flank a fireplace. A large island provides workspace in the kitchen, which is open to the breakfast nook. The master suite is on the left side of the house, while two bedrooms and one bath are on the right.

Rear Exterior

© Stephen Fuller, Inc.

Photography by Scott Moore, MWS Photography. This home, as shown in photographs, may differ from the actual blueprints. For more detailed information, please check the floor plans carefully.

HPK3600097

First Floor: 1,804 sq. ft.
Second Floor: 1,041 sq. ft.
Total: 2,845 sq. ft.
Bedrooms: 4
Bathrooms: 3 ½
Width: 57' - 3"
Depth: 71' - 0"
Foundation: Finished
Walkout Basement
Price Code: C4

Order online @ eplans.com

FOXBOROUGH HILL

There's a feeling of old Charleston in this stately home—particularly on the quiet side porch that wraps around the kitchen and breakfast room. The interior of this home revolves around a spacious great room with a welcoming fireplace. The left wing is dedicated to the master suite, which boasts wide views of the rear property. The kitchen easily serves the dining room and breakfast area. Three family bedrooms are tucked upstairs.

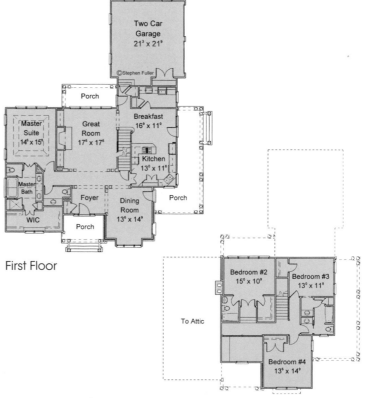

First Floor

Second Floor

218 HOLLY RIDGE

First Floor

Second Floor

HPK3600098

First Floor: 2,070 sq. ft.
Second Floor: 790 sq. ft.
Total: 2,860 sq. ft.
Bedrooms: 4
Bathrooms: 3 ½
Width: 58' - 4"
Depth: 54' - 10"
Foundation: Finished
Walkout Basement
Price Code: C4

Order online @ eplans.com

The striking combination of wood frame, shingles, and glass creates the exterior of this classic cottage. To the left of the foyer is a study with a warming hearth and vaulted ceiling. A great room with attached breakfast area is near the kitchen. A guest room is nestled in the rear of the plan for privacy. The master suite provides an expansive tray ceiling, glass sitting area, and easy passage to the outside deck. Upstairs, two bedrooms are accompanied by a loft for a quiet getaway.

© Stephen Fuller, Inc.

HPK3600099

First Floor: 2,070 sq. ft.
Second Floor: 790 sq. ft.
Total: 2,860 sq. ft.
Bedrooms: 4
Bathrooms: 3 ½
Width: 57' - 6"
Depth: 54' - 0"
Foundation: Finished
Walkout Basement
Price Code: C4

Order online @ eplans.com

CALAVERAS

First Floor

Wood shingles are a cozy touch on the exterior of this home. Interior rooms include a great room with a bay window and fireplace, a formal dining room, and a study with another fireplace. A guest room on the first floor contains a full bath and walk-in closet. The sumptuous master suite is on the first floor for privacy. The second floor holds two additional bedrooms, a loft area, and a gallery overlooking the central hall.

Second Floor

© Stephen Fuller, Inc.

CHESTNUT LANE

First Floor

Second Floor

HPK3600100

First Floor: 1,960 sq. ft.
Second Floor: 905 sq. ft.
Total: 2,865 sq. ft.
Bonus Space: 297 sq. ft.
Bedrooms: 4
Bathrooms: 3 ½
Width: 61' - 0"
Depth: 70' - 6"
Foundation: Finished
Walkout Basement
Price Code: C4

Order online @ eplans.com

Traditionalists will appreciate the classic styling of this Colonial home. The foyer opens to both a banquet-sized dining room and formal living room with a fireplace. The entire right side of the main level is taken up by the enchanting master suite. The left side includes a large kitchen and a breakfast room. Upstairs, each bedroom features ample closet space. The detached garage features an unfinished office or studio on its second level.

HPK3600101

First Floor: 1,944 sq. ft.
Second Floor: 954 sq. ft.
Total: 2,898 sq. ft.
Bedrooms: 4
Bathrooms: 3 ½
Width: 51' - 6"
Depth: 73' - 0"
Foundation: Unfinished Walkout Basement
Price Code: C4

Order online @ eplans.com

225 HOLLY RIDGE

This gracious home combines warm informal materials with a modern livable floor plan to create a true southern classic. The dining room, study, and great room work together to create one large, exciting space. Plenty of counter space and storage make the kitchen user friendly. The master suite is a welcome retreat. Upstairs, two additional bedrooms each have their own vanities within a shared bath; the third bedroom includes its own bath.

First Floor

Second Floor

© Stephen Fuller, Inc.

Ansley Park Home

First Floor

Second Floor

HPK3600102

First Floor: 1,870 sq. ft.
Second Floor: 1,030 sq. ft.
Total: 2,900 sq. ft.
Bonus Space: 294 sq. ft.
Bedrooms: 4
Bathrooms: 3 ½
Width: 50' - 9"
Depth: 66' - 0"
Foundation: Finished
Walkout Basement
Price Code: C4

Order online @ eplans.com

This picturesque home draws on many traditions, with intricate brick detailing, steeply pitched gables, and arched windows. Recessed double doors and a handsome clerestory add interest to the exterior. The soaring great room features a centered fireplace framed by a tall window and French doors. In the formal dining room, a triple window allows a view of the back property. The secluded first-floor master suite with a vaulted ceiling is complemented by three second-floor bedrooms and a loft overlooking the foyer.

© Stephen Fuller, Inc.

HPK3600103

First Floor: 2,076 sq. ft.
Second Floor: 843 sq. ft.
Total: 2,919 sq. ft.
Bedrooms: 4
Bathrooms: 3 ½
Width: 57' - 6"
Depth: 51' - 6"
Foundation: Finished
Walkout Basement
Price Code: C4

Order online @ eplans.com

WELCOME MEADOW

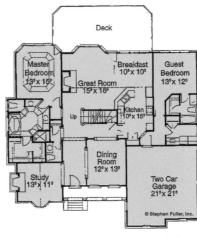

First Floor

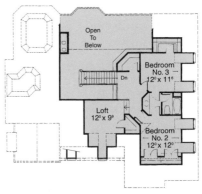

Second Floor

This lovely home's foyer opens to the formal dining room, defined by decorative columns, and leads to a two-story great room. The breakfast room joins the great room to create a casual family area. The master suite boasts a coffered ceiling and a sumptuous bath. A guest suite with a private bath is located just off the kitchen. Upstairs, two family bedrooms share a compartmented bath and a raised loft.

© Stephen Fuller, Inc.

Cayman

MASTER BATH
SITTING RM.
11'-6" X 10'-0"
DECK
KEEPING ROOM
15'-3" X 15'-3"
MASTER SUITE
18'-0" X 16'-0"
W.I.C.
GREAT ROOM
15'-6" X 17'-3"
KITCHEN
14'-0" X 13'-3"
BREAKFAST
14'-0" X 13'-0"
VLT. CLG.
DN.
BEDROOM NO. 3
12'-0" X 12'-0"
LAUNDRY
POWDER
W.I.C.
W.I.C.
FOYER
BATH
BEDROOM NO. 2
13'-3" X 11'-6"
DINING ROOM
13'-3" X 18'-6"
2-CAR GARAGE
21'-6" X 21'-6"
STOOP
VLT. CLG.
© Stephen Fuller, Inc.

HPK3600104

Square Footage: 2,935
Bedrooms: 3
Bathrooms: 2 ½
Width: 71' - 0"
Depth: 66' - 0"
Foundation: Finished
Walkout Basement
Price Code: C4

Order online @ eplans.com

This spacious one-story home easily accommodates a large family, providing all the luxuries and necessities for gracious living. For formal occasions, a grand dining room sits just off the entry foyer and features a vaulted ceiling. The great room offers a beautiful ceiling treatment and access to the rear deck. The spacious master suite is filled with amenities. Two family bedrooms share a full bath.

© Stephen Fuller, Inc.

HPK3600105

First Floor: 1,475 sq. ft.
Second Floor: 1,460 sq. ft.
Total: 2,935 sq. ft.
Bedrooms: 4
Bathrooms: 3 ½
Width: 57' - 6"
Depth: 46' - 6"
Foundation: Unfinished
Walkout Basement
Price Code: C4

Order online @ eplans.com

FANCREST

Quaint keystones and shutters offer charming accents to the siding-and-stone exterior of this stately English country home. The two-story foyer opens through decorative columns to the formal living room. The nearby media room shares a through-fireplace with the two-story great room. The left wing of the second floor is dedicated to the rambling master suite, which boasts angled walls, a tray ceiling, and a bayed sitting area.

First Floor

Second Floor

© Stephen Fuller, Inc.

HPK3600106

First Floor: 1,475 sq. ft.
Second Floor: 1,460 sq. ft.
Total: 2,935 sq. ft.
Bedrooms: 4
Bathrooms: 3 ½
Width: 57' - 6"
Depth: 46' - 6"
Foundation: Finished
Walkout Basement
Price Code: C4

Order online @ eplans.com

WATERFORD

First Floor

Second Floor

French doors open to a dining room with excellent frontal views, and to a living room that leads to a media room. The bayed great room offers access to the rear deck, for full enjoyment of outdoor activities. An island kitchen with a bayed breakfast nook completes the first floor. Upstairs, Bedrooms 2 and 3 share a full bath, and Bedroom 4 has its own bath. The master bedroom features a bayed sitting area and an exquisite master bath.

HPK3600107

First Floor: 1,581 sq. ft.

Second Floor: 1,415 sq. ft.

Total: 2,996 sq. ft.

Bedrooms: 4

Bathrooms: 3

Width: 55' - 0"

Depth: 52' - 0"

Foundation: Finished Walkout Basement

Price Code: C4

Order online @ eplans.com

229 WILLOW TRACE

First Floor

Classical details and a stately brick exterior accentuate the grace and timeless elegance of this home. The two-story great room awaits, featuring a wet bar and warming fireplace. To the left is the sunlit breakfast room and efficient kitchen. Upstairs, the master suite features a private deck, while two large family bedrooms offer separate vanities and share a bath.

Second Floor

© Stephen Fuller, Inc.

WELLINGTON

Deck

Master Bedroom 16⁰x19³

Great Room 17³x16⁰

Breakfast 14⁰x16⁰

Bedroom No. 2 12⁰x14³

Kitchen 14⁰x15³

Bedroom No. 3 12⁶x14⁰

Living Room 12⁹x14⁰

Foyer

Dining Room 13⁹x15⁶

Two Car Garage 21³x23⁶

Porch

© Stephen Fuller, Inc.

HPK3600108

Square Footage: 2,998
Bedrooms: 3
Bathrooms: 2 ½
Width: 75' - 6"
Depth: 57' - 0"
Foundation: Finished
Walkout Basement
Price Code: C4

Order online @ eplans.com

This Colonial adaptation enjoys classic details but insists on a distinctly contemporary interior. At the heart of this sophisticated floor plan lies the great room with French doors to the deck. The secluded master suite offers a private bath with twin lavatories and a walk-in closet with its own window. Each of the two family bedrooms offers a private door to a shared full bath.

HPK3600109

First Floor: 2,081 sq. ft.
Second Floor: 940 sq. ft.
Total: 3,021 sq. ft.
Bedrooms: 4
Bathrooms: 3 ½
Width: 69' - 9"
Depth: 65' - 0"
Foundation: Finished
Walkout Basement
Price Code: L1

Order online @ eplans.com

PROVIDENCE

First Floor

Second Floor

From its pediment to the columned porch, this Georgian facade is impressive. Inside, classical symmetry balances the living and dining rooms on either side of the foyer. The two-story great room features built-in cabinetry, a fireplace, and a large bay window. The island kitchen opens to the breakfast area. The master suite boasts a tray ceiling, a wall of glass, and access to the rear deck as well as a private bath.

© Stephen Fuller, Inc.
© Stephen Fuller, Inc.

ANDREAS

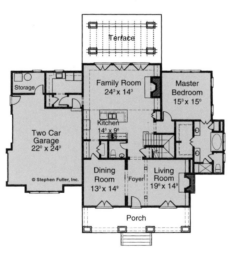

First Floor

Second Floor

This lovely Craftsman-style home invites enjoyment of the outdoors with a front covered porch and a spacious rear terrace. Inside, formal rooms flank the foyer and feature lovely amenities such as French-door access to the front porch. A fireplace warms the family room, which provides plenty of natural light and wide views through three sets of glass doors. Additional bedrooms on the second floor enjoy a balcony overlook to the family room.

© Stephen Fuller, Inc.

HPK3600111

First Floor: 1,370 sq. ft.

Second Floor: 1,673 sq. ft.

Total: 3,043 sq. ft.

Bedrooms: 4

Bathrooms: 3 ½

Width: 73' - 6"

Depth: 49' - 0"

Foundation: Finished
Walkout Basement

Price Code: C4

Order online @ eplans.com

This English Georgian home features a dramatic brick exterior. The series of windows and Jack-arch detailing are second only to the drama created by the porte cochere. Enter into the two-story foyer where the unusually shaped staircase and balcony create a tremendous first impression. Separated only by a classical colonnade detail, the living and dining rooms are perfect for entertaining. A guest room, a children's den area, two family bedrooms, and a master suite are upstairs.

213 WILLOW TRACE

First Floor

Second Floor

© Stephen Fuller, Inc.

WALDEN

BREAKFAST
12'-10" X 9'-0"

KITCHEN
16'-0" X 15'-8"

FAMILY ROOM
18'-0" X 15'-6"

DINING ROOM
13'-0" X 14'-10"

UP

LNDR.

DN

PWD.

LIVING ROOM
13'-0" X 14'-10"

TWO STORY
FOYER
13'-10" X 10'-4"

UP

STOOP

TWO CAR GARAGE
20'-10" X 21'-4"

© Stephen Fuller, Inc.

First Floor

SITTING ROOM
12'-10" X 9'-0"

MASTER BEDROOM
17'-0" X 15'-6"

BATH

BEDROOM NO. 4
11'-10" X 11'-8"

BEDROOM NO. 3
11'-1" X 10'-6"

BATH

MASTER BATH

HIS

ON. DN.

OPEN TO BELOW

BEDROOM NO. 2
11'-2" X 10'-6"

HERS

EXERCISE
9'-0" X 6'-6"

UNFIN.
14'-10" X 6'-6"

Second Floor

HPK3600112

First Floor: 1,530 sq. ft.
Second Floor: 1,515 sq. ft.
Total: 3,045 sq. ft.
Bedrooms: 4
Bathrooms: 3 ½
Width: 49' - 8"
Depth: 57' - 4"
Foundation: Finished
Walkout Basement
Price Code: L1

Order online @ eplans.com

The French Country charm of this home is irresistible, with its gambrel roof, use of stone and wood, and segmented-stone arch windows. The living room features a fireplace; columns present the adjacent dining room. The kitchen includes a work island and a breakfast room that opens to the family room with fireplace and wet bar. Upstairs, the hallway leads to two bedrooms, both with large closets. A fourth bedroom has a private bath. The master suite includes a bayed sitting area, luxurious master bath, and exercise room.

HPK3600113

Square Footage: 3,063
Bedrooms: 3
Bathrooms: 3 ½
Width: 68' - 0"
Depth: 80' - 0"
Foundation: Finished
Walkout Basement
Price Code: L1

Order online @ eplans.com

LAUREL LANE

Although all on one level, the floor plan for this home defines masterful design. The great room and dining room are separated only by well-placed columns, yet each is distinct in its purpose and structure. Similarly, the keeping room is open to the breakfast area and kitchen, but retains a sense of solitude with a cozy fireplace and built-ins. The kitchen is a gourmet's dream, with a huge storage pantry, butler's pantry, and an island cooktop. Each bedroom has its own bath. Reach the covered porch via the great room, keeping room, or master bedroom.

© Stephen Fuller, Inc.

MAGNOLIA PLACE

First Floor

Second Floor

HPK3600114

First Floor: 1,455 sq. ft.
Second Floor: 1,649 sq. ft.
Total: 3,104 sq. ft.
Bedrooms: 4
Bathrooms: 3 ½
Width: 54' - 4"
Depth: 46' - 0"
Foundation: Finished
Walkout Basement
Price Code: L1

Order online @ eplans.com

The double wings, twin chimneys, and center portico of this home work in concert to create a classic architectural statement. The two-story foyer is flanked by the spacious dining room and formal living room, each containing its own fireplace. A large family room with a full wall of glass opens conveniently to the kitchen and breakfast room. The master suite features a tray ceiling and French doors that open to a covered porch.

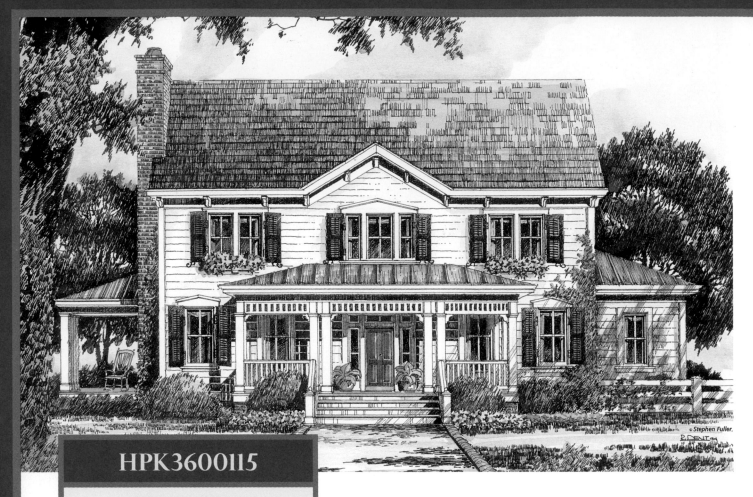

HPK3600115

First Floor: 1,613 sq. ft.
Second Floor: 1,546 sq. ft.
Total: 3,159 sq. ft.
Bedrooms: 4
Bathrooms: 3 ½
Width: 69' - 0"
Depth: 57' - 0"
Foundation: Finished
Walkout Basement
Price Code: L1

Order online @ eplans.com

CUSHING MEADOWS

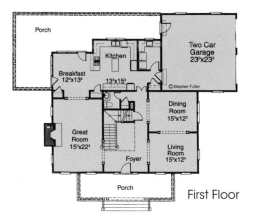

First Floor

Second Floor

This new design wears the timeless appeal of classic country style, but gives it a fresh face. A low-pitched roof complements the columns and balusters of the front covered porch. Formal areas are secluded to one side of the plan, while the family room, kitchen, and breakfast area have open interior space and views of the rear property. The master suite boasts a windowside tub and twin lavatories. Each of two family bedrooms has private access to a shared bath, while a fourth offers its own full bath.

© Stephen Fuller, Inc.

CORAL KEEP

First Floor

Second Floor

HPK3600116

First Floor: 2,155 sq. ft.
Second Floor: 1,020 sq. ft.
Total: 3,175 sq. ft.
Bedrooms: 4
Bathrooms: 3 ½
Width: 62' - 0"
Depth: 63' - 0"
Foundation: Unfinished
Walkout Basement
Price Code: C4

Order online @ eplans.com

To highlight the exterior of this home, wood siding and paneled shutters artfully combine with arched transoms and a sweeping roofline. Double doors open to the master suite with its warming fireplace. The exercise room can be accessed from the master bedroom or the great room. The cooktop-island kitchen includes a pantry and a laundry room. The second-floor gallery features built-in bookshelves, and a computer/study nook easily accessible from all three bedrooms on the upper level.

© Stephen Fuller, Inc.

HPK3600117

First Floor: 2,502 sq. ft.
Second Floor: 677 sq. ft.
Total: 3,179 sq. ft.
Bonus Space: 171 sq. ft.
Bedrooms: 4
Bathrooms: 3 ½
Width: 71' - 2"
Depth: 56' - 10"
Foundation: Finished
Walkout Basement
Price Code: L1

Order online @ eplans.com

Stone and stucco bring a chateau welcome to this Mediterranean-style home. A sensational sunroom lights up the rear of the plan and flows to the bayed breakfast nook. A coffered ceiling and columned archways decorate the living area, which opens to the formal dining room. A master suite with rear-deck access leads to a family or guest bedroom with a private bath. Upstairs, two secondary bedrooms and a full bath enjoy easy kitchen access down a side stairway.

CARA VISTA

First Floor

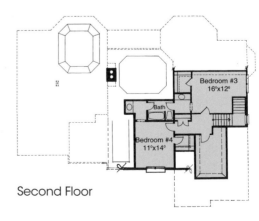

Second Floor

© Stephen Fuller, Inc.

AVALLON ESTATES

Deck

Breakfast/
Sun Room
12⁶ x 10⁰

Great
Room
16⁰ x 19⁶

Kitchen
12⁶ x 15⁰

Master
Suite
16⁰ x 18⁰

Master
Bath

Option
Room
12⁰ x 13⁶

Foyer

Dining
Room
12⁰ x 17⁰

Stoop

Two Car
Garage
23⁰ x 21⁰

© Stephen Fuller, Inc.

First Floor

Open To
Below

Child's Den
Bedroom #4
12⁶ x 13⁰

Play Area
/ Loft
8⁰ x 8⁰

Bedroom
#2
12⁰ x 15⁰

Bedroom
#3
11⁰ x 16⁰

© Stephen Fuller, Inc.

Second Floor

HPK3600118

First Floor: 2,067 sq. ft.
Second Floor: 1,129 sq. ft.
Total: 3,196 sq. ft.
Bedrooms: 4
Bathrooms: 4
Width: 69' - 0"
Depth: 63' - 0"
Foundation: Unfinished
Walkout Basement
Price Code: L1

Order online @ eplans.com

This French chateau boasts all the charm of Europe and features all the modern conveniences for today's busy lifestyles. Inside, the foyer is flanked by the formal dining room and an optional room perfect for a guest suite, connecting to a hall bath. The great room is truly magnificent, with an enormous hearth and two sets of double doors opening onto the rear porch. The kitchen connects to a breakfast/sunroom for casual family dining.

HPK3600119

First Floor: 1,570 sq. ft.
Second Floor: 1,630 sq. ft.
Total: 3,200 sq. ft.
Bedrooms: 4
Bathrooms: 3 ½
Width: 59' - 10"
Depth: 43' - 4"
Foundation: Finished
Walkout Basement
Price Code: L1

Order online @ eplans.com

HIGHPOINT

First Floor

This classic Americana design employs wood siding, a variety of window styles, and a detailed front porch. Inside, the large two-story foyer flows into the formal dining room with arched window accents and the living room highlighted by a bay window. A short passage with a wet bar accesses the family room with its wall of windows, French doors, and fireplace. The large breakfast area and open island kitchen are spacious and airy as well as efficient.

Second Floor

© Stephen Fuller, Inc.

DUNWOODY CLASSIC

HPK3600120

First Floor: 1,554 sq. ft.
Second Floor: 1,648 sq. ft.
Total: 3,202 sq. ft.
Bedrooms: 4
Bathrooms: 3 ½
Width: 60' - 0"
Depth: 43' - 0"
Foundation: Finished
Walkout Basement
Price Code: L1

Order online @ eplans.com

First Floor

The classic styling of this brick American traditional home will be respected for years to come. The formidable double-door entry with a transom and a Palladian window reveals the shining foyer within. A large family room with a full wall of glass conveniently opens to the breakfast room and kitchen.

Second Floor

HPK3600121

First Floor: 1,683 sq. ft.
Second Floor: 1,544 sq. ft.
Total: 3,227 sq. ft.
Bonus Space: 176 sq. ft.
Bedrooms: 5
Bathrooms: 4
Width: 60' - 0"
Depth: 48' - 6"
Foundation: Finished
Walkout Basement
Price Code: L1

Order online @ eplans.com

230 MAGNOLIA PLACE

First Floor

Second Floor

This country cottage's stucco exterior, mixed with stone and shingles, creates a warmth that is accented with a fan-light transom. The two-story foyer opens onto the staircase and then flows easily into the dining room, living room, and family room. The great room features a fireplace and bookcases and opens to a well-lit breakfast and kitchen area. Upstairs are three additional bedrooms and space for a bonus or play room. The master suite features a tray ceiling, sitting area and a lush master bath.

© Stephen Fuller, Inc.

220 WILLOW TRACE

First Floor

Second Floor

HPK3600122

First Floor: 1,450 sq. ft.
Second Floor: 1,795 sq. ft.
Total: 3,245 sq. ft.
Bedrooms: 4
Bathrooms: 3 ½
Width: 61' - 5"
Depth: 49' - 0"
Foundation: Finished
Walkout Basement
Price Code: L1

Order online @ eplans.com

Stucco and stone with cedar shingle accents make this country cottage uniquely captivating. The great room is the central gathering place and includes a fireplace. A wraparound porch opens both to the family room and the breakfast room, serving as a warm-weather extension of living space. Up the angled staircase, two bedrooms share a bath with dual sinks, and another accesses a private bath. Across the balcony, the dramatic master suite is highlighted by a fireplace and private second-floor porch.

© Stephen Fuller, Inc.

HPK3600123

First Floor: 1,811 sq. ft.
Second Floor: 1,437 sq. ft.
Total: 3,248 sq. ft.
Bonus Space: 286 sq. ft.
Bedrooms: 4
Bathrooms: 4
Width: 53' - 6"
Depth: 60' - 6"
Foundation: Finished
Walkout Basement
Price Code: L1

Order online @ eplans.com

NORTH HIGHLANDS

Topping the arched entry of this home is a lovely transom window, which admits sunlight to enhance the two-story foyer. The formal living and dining rooms are brought together by a through-fireplace. Generously sized windows in these rooms allow views of the surrounding property. An additional fireplace is in the corner of the keeping room, adjacent to the kitchen and the breakfast area. The master suite features an expansive master bath with a large walk-in closet.

First Floor

Second Floor

© Stephen Fuller, Inc.

HERITAGE VIEW

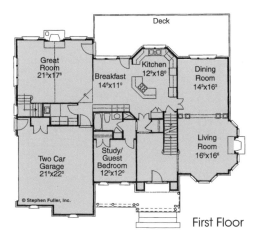

First Floor

Second Floor

HPK3600124

First Floor: 1,888 sq. ft.
Second Floor: 1,374 sq. ft.
Total: 3,262 sq. ft.
Bonus Space: 299 sq. ft.
Bedrooms: 3
Bathrooms: 3
Width: 63' - 0"
Depth: 49' - 0"
Foundation: Finished
Walkout Basement
Price Code: L1

Order online @ eplans.com

This Colonial home speaks of a graceful era. A formal living room with bay window and fireplace joins the dining room with stately columns. The gourmet kitchen has a uniquely angled countertop and a breakfast area. The two-story great room is appointed with a fireplace, a media corner, and a rear staircase. Upstairs, tray ceilings adorn the master suite's bedroom and bath. Two additional bedrooms and a full bath complete the sleeping quarters.

© Stephen Fuller, Inc.

HPK3600125

First Floor: 1,700 sq. ft.
Second Floor: 1,585 sq. ft.
Total: 3,285 sq. ft.
Bonus Space: 176 sq. ft.
Bedrooms: 5
Bathrooms: 4
Width: 60' - 0"
Depth: 47' - 6"
Foundation: Finished
Walkout Basement
Price Code: L1

Order online @ eplans.com

SOUTHWIND

The front porch of this two-story farm-house opens to a traditional foyer flanked by the formal areas. For casual family living, a great room with a fireplace and a kitchen with a breakfast area will serve the family's needs. Upstairs, the master suite contains a bayed sitting area and a private bath. A rear deck complements the inviting front porch in this spacious design.

First Floor

Second Floor

© Stephen Fuller, Inc.

DRUID HILLS MANOR

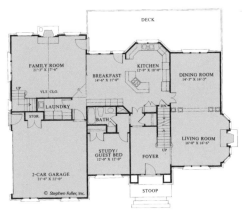

First Floor

Second Floor

HPK3600126

First Floor: 1,847 sq. ft.
Second Floor: 1,453 sq. ft.
Total: 3,300 sq. ft.
Bedrooms: 4
Bathrooms: 3
Width: 63' - 3"
Depth: 47' - 0"
Foundation: Unfinished
Walkout Basement
Price Code: L1

Order online @ eplans.com

This elegant manor features a dramatic brick exterior highlighted with a varied roofline and a finial atop the uppermost gable. The plan opens to a two-story foyer, with formal rooms on the right; the living room fireplace is set in a bay window. The more casual family room is to the rear. For guests, a bedroom and bath are located on the main level. The second floor provides additional bedrooms and baths for family as well as a magnificent master suite.

©Stephen Fuller, Inc.

HPK3600127

First Floor: 2,355 sq. ft.
Second Floor: 987 sq. ft.
Total: 3,342 sq. ft.
Bedrooms: 4
Bathrooms: 3 ½
Width: 61' - 6"
Depth: 52' - 6"
Foundation: Finished
Walkout Basement
Price Code: L1

Order online @ eplans.com

139 KENNESAW COUNTRY

First Floor

Second Floor

The front of this traditional home is characterized by the arch pattern evident in the windows, doorway, and above the columned front porch. The master suite includes a vaulted study that opens from the foyer. The study's two-sided fireplace also warms the bedroom. Through the master suite and beyond two walk-in closets is a bath with dual vanities. Upstairs are three more bedrooms and two full baths.

© Stephen Fuller, Inc.

224 Magnolia Place

First Floor

Second Floor

HPK3600128

First Floor: 1,678 sq. ft.
Second Floor: 1,677 sq. ft.
Total: 3,355 sq. ft.
Bedrooms: 4
Bathrooms: 3 ½
Width: 50' - 0"
Depth: 50' - 6"
Foundation: Finished
Walkout Basement
Price Code: L1

Order online @ eplans.com

This English manor home features a dramatic brick-and-stucco exterior. Inside, the foyer opens to the formal living room accented with a vaulted ceiling and box-bay window. The dining room features its own angled bay window. An entire wall of glass, accented by a central fireplace, spans from the family room to the breakfast area and kitchen. For guests, a bedroom and bath are located on the main level. The second floor provides two additional bedrooms and a bath. The master suite is a pleasant retreat.

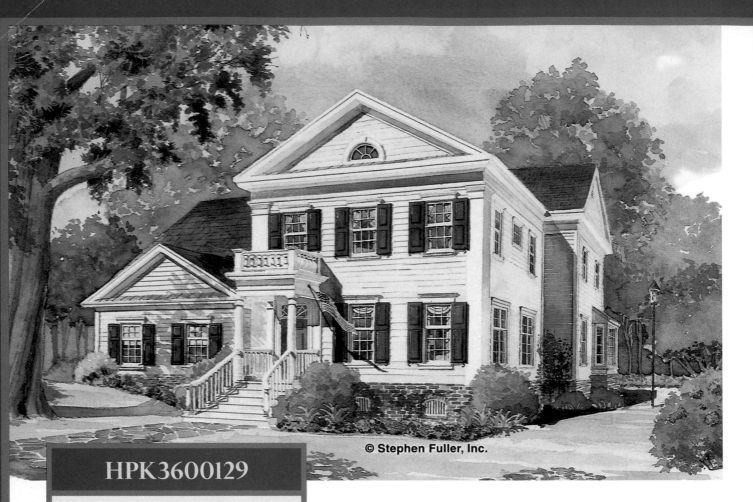

© Stephen Fuller, Inc.

HPK3600129

First Floor: 1,959 sq. ft.
Second Floor: 1,408 sq. ft.
Total: 3,367 sq. ft.
Bedrooms: 4
Bathrooms: 3 ½
Width: 61' - 9"
Depth: 62' - 9"
Foundation: Finished
Walkout Basement
Price Code: L1

Order online @ eplans.com

343 WOODBURY

An elegant front entrance welcomes you to this classically styled home. Enjoy the interior fireplace, or use the French doors to go out onto the rear covered porch. An island kitchen is convenient to both the dining room and a sunny breakfast room. Guests will be grateful for the privacy of the guest bedroom and access to the porch. The family sleeping zone is upstairs and includes a master suite with fireplace and deluxe bath plus two secondary bedrooms and an unfinished open space for future expansion.

First Floor

Second Floor

© Stephen Fuller, Inc

Avignon

First Floor

Second Floor

HPK3600130

First Floor: 2,357 sq. ft.
Second Floor: 1,021 sq. ft.
Total: 3,378 sq. ft.
Bonus Space: 168 sq. ft.
Bedrooms: 4
Bathrooms: 3 ½
Width: 70' - 0"
Depth: 62' - 6"
Foundation: Finished
Walkout Basement
Price Code: L1

Order online @ eplans.com

Here, the basic formality of the Chateau style has been purposely mellowed for modern-day living. A quaint keeping room with a fire-place adjoins the kitchen and breakfast areas. Upstairs, find three generous bedrooms and two baths plus a bonus room.

© Stephen Fuller, Inc.

HPK3600131

First Floor: 1,621 sq. ft.
Second Floor: 1,766 sq. ft.
Total: 3,387 sq. ft.
Bedrooms: 4
Bathrooms: 3 ½
Width: 52' - 0"
Depth: 50' - 6"
Foundation: Finished
Walkout Basement
Price Code: L1

Order online @ eplans.com

STRATFORD PLACE

First Floor

All-American charm springs from the true Colonial style of this distinguished home. Double French doors partition the casual region of the home, which features the comfortable family room and its lovely fireplace. A guest room is located behind the kitchen area, making it a perfect maid's or nurse's room. The master suite has a private study, a fireplace, and an amenity-laden bath with an extended walk-in closet. Two additional bedrooms share a private, compartmented bath.

Second Floor

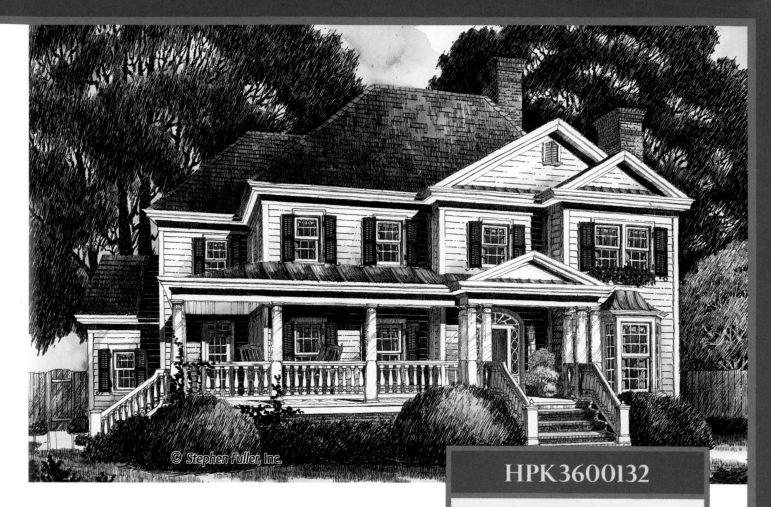
© Stephen Fuller, Inc.

GRAYSON

First Floor

Second Floor

HPK3600132

First Floor: 1,780 sq. ft.
Second Floor: 1,668 sq. ft.
Total: 3,448 sq. ft.
Bedrooms: 4
Bathrooms: 4
Width: 53' - 0"
Depth: 57' - 3"
Foundation: Unfinished
Walkout Basement
Price Code: L1

Order online @ eplans.com

This Colonial-minded country home shows a robust streetside elevation that features a wide porch, pedimented entry, and side-loading garage. Besides the formal dining room at the front of the plan, the layout is casual. Upstairs bedrooms are also full suites and well separated for privacy. The master bedroom is adorned by a tray ceiling and accesses an exclusive deck.

© Stephen Fuller, Inc.

Photo by Dave Dawson. This home, as shown in photographs, may differ from the actual blueprints. For more detailed information, please check the floor plans carefully.

HPK3600133

First Floor: 2,208 sq. ft.
Second Floor: 1,250 sq. ft.
Total: 3,458 sq. ft.
Bedrooms: 4
Bathrooms: 3 ½
Width: 60' - 6"
Depth: 60' - 0"
Foundation: Finished
Walkout Basement
Price Code: L1

Order online @ eplans.com

PEACHTREE PLACE

First Floor

Second Floor

Quaint yet majestic, this European-style home has the enchantment of arched windows to underscore its charm. The foyer leads through French doors to the study with its own hearth and coffered ceiling. The master suite features a tray ceiling and large, accommodating bath. The sunken great room is highlighted by a fireplace, built-in bookcases, lots of glass, and easy access to a back stair and gourmet kitchen. Three secondary bedrooms reside upstairs. One upstairs bedroom offers guests a private bath and walk-in closet.

144   STEPHEN FULLER'S TRADITIONAL HOME

ORDER BLUEPRINTS ANYTIME AT EPLANS.COM OR 1-800-521-6797

© Stephen Fuller, Inc.

CAMP HILL

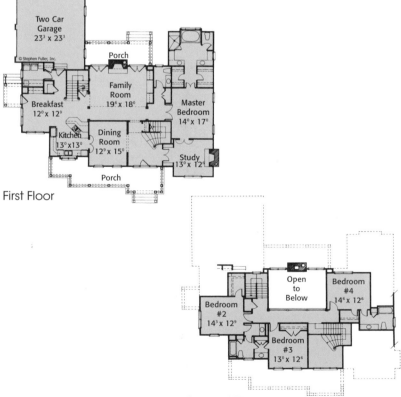

First Floor

- Two Car Garage 23³ x 23⁵
- Porch
- Breakfast 12⁰ x 12⁹
- Family Room 19⁶ x 18⁰
- Master Bedroom 14⁰ x 17⁰
- Kitchen 13⁰ x13⁰
- Dining Room 12⁹ x 15⁰
- Study 13⁰ x 12⁰
- Porch

Second Floor

- Bedroom #2 14³ x 12⁹
- Open to Below
- Bedroom #4 14⁶ x 12⁶
- Bedroom #3 13⁰ x 12⁶

HPK3600134

First Floor: 2,360 sq. ft.
Second Floor: 1,133 sq. ft.
Total: 3,493 sq. ft.
Bedrooms: 4
Bathrooms: 3 ½
Width: 68' - 0"
Depth: 62' - 5"
Foundation: Unfinished Walkout Basement
Price Code: L1

Order online @ eplans.com

Farmhouse life has never been as good as it is in this two-story classic. The foyer opens to a fanned staircase, but all of the common rooms are on the first floor. The kitchen's peninsula snack bar separates it from the nook and faces the nearby family room. A second set of stairs leads down to an unfinished walk-out basement or up to the second floor, where there are three bedrooms and two baths. The master suite remains quiet and secluded on the first floor.

La Maison De Rêves

An impeccably detailed home from the Norman countryside

Photo by B. Massey Photographers. This home, as shown in photographs, may differ from the actual blueprints. For more detailed information, please check the floor plans carefully.

ABOVE: Wrought-iron details and a prominent archway keep the two-story height of the foyer from feeling trivial.

Derived from a classic French vocabulary, this distinctive design provides a cohesive, refined disposition and charming character in every detail. Inspired by the architecture of the French Eclectic style, La Maison de Rêves features a stone-and-brick facade, punctuated inside by a satisfying iteration of antique details.

Crosscut travertine floors, arched stacked-stone walls, and a winding wrought-iron staircase give the spacious foyer an elegant Old World flavor. The nearby dining room, with gold-leafed ceiling and full-height windows, is appropriate for very formal affairs. A gracefully arched entry introduces the great room, the centerpiece of which is a stone fireplace flanked by built-ins.

Head left where wrought-iron gate guards a lovely wine niche and, just beyond, the gourmet kitchen. Distressed brick flooring, a fireplace, and exposed-beam ceilings bring charm to this French Country space. The accompanying breakfast area includes floor-to-ceiling windows that bring light and a seasonal sense to the indoors. Just beyond, the keeping room features an impressive stone fireplace that imparts a medieval flavor to the room.

An appreciation of style, space, and efficiency is showcased in the dramatic master suite, complete with a fireplace, sitting area, and lavishly draped windows. Tall windows frame the hearth, and a door leads out to a private area of the rear porch. The luxurious bath provides a soft color palette, two walk-in closets, separate vanities, and a sunken tub.

LEFT: Segmented arches, each with a keystone detail, establish a robust formalism in the great room.

BELOW: The large roof, arched windows and entries, and asymmetrical facade are details from the home's French inspiration.

On the second floor, a gallery overlooking the foyer leads to the family's sleeping quarters. Each of the secondary bedrooms has separate access to a full bath and plenty of wardrobe space. A bonus room offers the possibility of a computer nook, home office, or play room. Finish the plan with a creative landscape package with a centrally controlled irrigation system and site lighting, and be the envy of your neighborhood.

LEFT: The home's other fireplace occasions a casual and elegant gathering area for the family.

BELOW: Matching built-in shelves surround and help bring focus to the fireplace.

Keeping Rm.
14⁰ x 21⁰

Covered Porch

Sitting Area
14⁹ x 9⁰

Breakfast
11⁰ x 13⁰

Wine Cellar

Great Room
19⁶ x 17⁹

Master Suite
18⁰ x 14⁶

Kitchen
21⁰ x 11⁶

Laundry

Dining Rm
12⁹ x 15⁶

Foyer

Hers

His

Master Bath

© Stephen Fuller, Inc.

Stoop

3 Car Garage
21⁰ x 30³

First Floor

Bedroom No. 4 /Office
12⁰ x 11⁹

Bedroom No. 3
12⁰ x 15⁶

Media Rm
18⁰ x 17⁹

Attic Storage

Gallery

Bedroom No. 2
12⁹ x 12⁶

Two Story Foyer

Bonus Room
9³ x 22³

Second Floor

HPK3600135

First Floor: 2,844 sq. ft.
Second Floor: 1,443 sq. ft.
Total: 4,287 sq. ft.
Bonus Space: 360 sq. ft.
Bedrooms: 4
Bathrooms: 4 ½
Width: 72' - 0"
Depth: 78' - 6"
Foundation: Unfinished Walkout Basement
Price Code: L2

Order online @ eplans.com

LEFT: Exposed beams adorn the rustic-style kitchen, perfectly finished here in wood and stone.

© Stephen Fuller, Inc.

HPK3600136

First Floor: 2,461 sq. ft.
Second Floor: 1,114 sq. ft.
Total: 3,575 sq. ft.
Bedrooms: 4
Bathrooms: 3 ½
Width: 84' - 4"
Depth: 63' - 0"
Foundation: Finished
Walkout Basement
Price Code: L1

Order online @ eplans.com

CARRINGTON HILLS

First Floor

Second Floor

A myriad of glass and ornamental stucco detailing complement the asymmetrical facade of this two-story home. Inside, an efficient L-shaped kitchen and bayed breakfast nook are conveniently located near the dining area. The living room opens through double doors to the rear terrace. The private master suite provides access to the rear terrace and adjacent study. The second floor contains three large bedrooms.

Santa Rosa Canyon

Breakfast
13⁹x14⁶

Terrace

Kitchen
13⁹x12⁹

Great Room
22⁰x17³

Dining
Room
14⁰x14⁰

Foyer

Living/
Study
15³x15⁹

Terrace

Two Car
Garage
22⁶x27⁶

© Stephen Fuller, Inc.

First Floor

Balcony

Master
Bedroom
22⁰x14⁶

W.I.C.

Bedroom
#3
14⁰x11⁶

Sitting
Area

Bedroom
#2
15³x15⁹

Second Floor

© Stephen Fuller, Inc

HPK3600137

First Floor: 1,900 sq. ft.
Second Floor: 1,676 sq. ft.
Total: 3,576 sq. ft.
Bedrooms: 3
Bathrooms: 3 ½
Width: 67' - 0"
Depth: 82' - 6"
Foundation: Crawlspace
Price Code: L1

Order online @ eplans.com

Gorgeous from any angle, this Mediterranean villa will delight and inspire. Enter from the front terrace to the foyer or through French doors to the dining room. Access the rear terrace from the great room, which is conveniently near the kitchen and breakfast nook. Upstairs, two bedrooms, each with its own bath, share a sitting area. A lavish bath and wraparound balcony make the master retreat a true haven.

HPK3600138

First Floor: 2,670 sq. ft.
Second Floor: 980 sq. ft.
Total: 3,650 sq. ft.
Bedrooms: 3
Bathrooms: 3 ½
Width: 64' - 7"
Depth: 78' - 0"
Foundation: Unfinished
Walkout Basement
Price Code: L1

Order online @ eplans.com

CANEY BRANCH

First Floor

Second Floor

The beautiful curved staircase is reminiscent of a true southern manor. The spacious dining room is adorned with cased openings and direct access to the expansive front porch. Arched built-in bookshelves line two walls and create ample storage and display space. A media room off the keeping room is sure to please. A tray ceiling distinguishes the master suite.

AMHERST

First Floor

Second Floor

HPK3600139

First Floor: 2,387 sq. ft.
Second Floor: 1,308 sq. ft.
Total: 3,695 sq. ft.
Bedrooms: 4
Bathrooms: 3 ½
Width: 76' - 6"
Depth: 51' - 6"
Foundation: Unfinished Basement
Price Code: L1

Order online @ eplans.com

This impressive stone house, with contrasting gables and interesting window treatments, has plenty of curb appeal. Centrally located, the great room will be the focus of most family activities, with its warming fireplace, built-in shelves, and French doors to the rear deck. An efficient kitchen and a sunny breakfast nook are nearby. Located on the ground floor for privacy, the sumptuous master suite includes an interesting ceiling, a large walk-in closet, and a pampering bath. Three family bedrooms and attic storage are available on the second floor.

© Stephen Fuller, Inc.

HPK3600140

First Floor: 2,569 sq. ft.
Second Floor: 1,128 sq. ft.
Total: 3,697 sq. ft.
Bonus Space: 339 sq. ft.
Bedrooms: 5
Bathrooms: 4
Width: 63' - 0"
Depth: 70' - 0"
Foundation: Unfinished
Walkout Basement
Price Code: L1

Order online @ eplans.com

St Germain

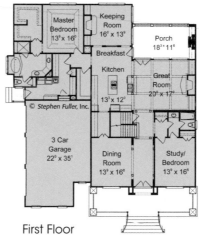
© Stephen Fuller, Inc.

Master Bedroom 13⁹ x 16⁰
Keeping Room 16⁰ x 13⁹
Porch 18³ x 11⁶
Breakfast
Kitchen 13³ x 12⁰
Great Room 20⁰ x 17⁰
3 Car Garage 22⁰ x 35'
Dining Room 13⁹ x 16⁰
Study/Bedroom 13⁹ x 16⁰

First Floor

Gently arched door and window openings soften the formal facade of this French Country home. The symmetry of the exterior is matched by a pair of rooms flanking the entry hall. A butler's pantry leads back to the island kitchen, which opens to the great room, breakfast area, and keeping room, lending a more open and informal feel to the rear half of the home.

© Stephen Fuller, Inc.

Unfinished Bonus Room 11⁰ x 17⁶
Bedroom #3 12 x 13
Bedroom #1 14³ x 12³
Bedroom #2 13⁹ x 12³

Second Floor

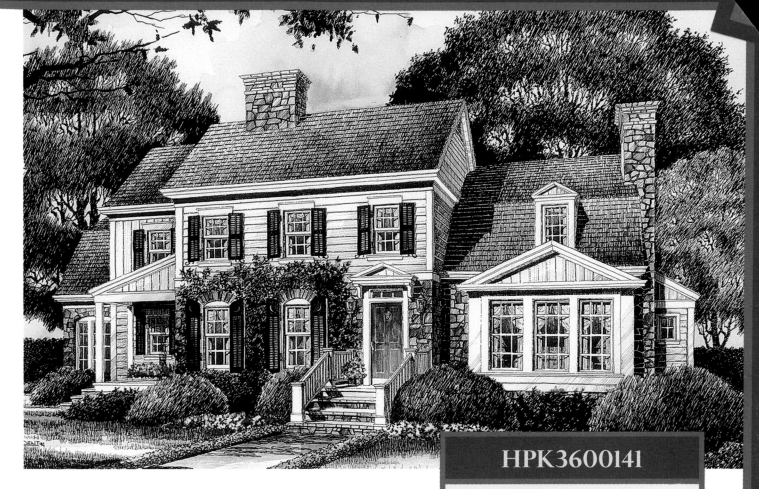

HOLLY BLUFF

Two Car
Garage
23⁰ x 26⁹

© Stephen Fuller, Inc.

Porch

Master
Bedroom
14⁶ x 20⁰

Breakfast
9⁶ x 13⁰

Great
Room
16⁶ x 17⁶

Kitchen
11⁹ x 14⁶

UP   DN

Dining
Room
16³ x 13⁶

Study
13⁰ x 13⁶

First Floor

Bonus
Room
13⁶ x 33⁰

© Stephen Fuller, Inc.

Bedroom
#2
13³ x 13⁹

Open To
Below

DN

Bedroom
#4
14³ x 13⁰

Open
To
Below

Bedroom
#3
16⁶ x 13³

Second Floor

HPK3600141

First Floor: 2,390 sq. ft.
Second Floor: 1,310 sq. ft.
Total: 3,700 sq. ft.
Bonus Space: 540 sq. ft.
Bedrooms: 4
Bathrooms: 3 ½
Width: 73' - 3"
Depth: 88' - 3"
Foundation: Unfinished
Walkout Basement
Price Code: L1

Order online @ eplans.com

Multiple entries and a side gambrel roof are features of farmhouse design. Here, they're updated with a two-car garage, two-story great room, and deluxe master suite. Formal elements at the front of the plan, such as the dining room and study, bring a well-mannered feeling to the home. The casual rooms, toward the back, add relaxing comfort. Don't miss the pampering master suite, with long master bath and private access to the study, wet bar, and rear porch.

HPK3600142

First Floor: 1,925 sq. ft.
Second Floor: 1,863 sq. ft.
Total: 3,788 sq. ft.
Bedrooms: 5
Bathrooms: 4
Width: 67' - 0"
Depth: 50' - 0"
Foundation: Unfinished
Walkout Basement
Price Code: L1

Order online @ eplans.com

KENNSINGTON

First Floor

With a touch of European style, the English country facade of this home is both enchanting and captivating. The rear of the first-floor plan features a guest room, a two-story great room with a fireplace, a large island kitchen, and a breakfast room overlooking the rear deck. Upstairs, an enticing master suite pampers the homeowner. Two family bedrooms share a full bath, while Bedroom 2 offers its own bath and walk-in closet.

Second Floor

© Stephen Fuller, Inc.

MANVILLE COURT

First Floor

Second Floor

HPK3600143

First Floor: 2,895 sq. ft.
Second Floor: 945 sq. ft.
Total: 3,840 sq. ft.
Bonus Space: 305 sq. ft.
Bedrooms: 4
Bathrooms: 3 ½
Width: 70' - 8"
Depth: 85' - 2"
Foundation: Unfinished
Walkout Basement
Price Code: L1

Order online @ eplans.com

Designed with a narrow lot in mind, the courtyard garage creates privacy from neighbors while also saving space. A front porch with square columns adds to the strength of this elevation. Enjoy alfresco meals on the screened porch off the keeping room. The sunroom off the dining room is a unique feature—great for entertaining. Bookshelves in the great room flank the fireplace. French doors add symmetry to the room.

HPK3600144

First Floor: 2,565 sq. ft.

Second Floor: 1,375 sq. ft.

Total: 3,940 sq. ft.

Bedrooms: 4

Bathrooms: 3 ½

Width: 88' - 6"

Depth: 58' - 6"

Foundation: Finished
Walkout Basement

Price Code: L1

Order online @ eplans.com

BROADWINGS

First Floor

Second Floor

A symmetrical facade with twin chimneys makes a grand statement. A covered porch welcomes visitors and provides a pleasant place to spend a mild evening. The entry foyer is flanked by formal living areas—a dining room and a living room—each with a fireplace. A third fireplace is the highlight of the expansive great room to the rear. An L-shaped kitchen offers a work island and a walk-in pantry, and easily serves the nearby breakfast nook and sunroom. The master suite provides lavish luxuries.

© Stephen Fuller, Inc.

NANTUCKET TRACE

HPK3600145

First Floor: 2,832 sq. ft.
Second Floor: 1,394 sq. ft.
Total: 4,226 sq. ft.
Bonus Space: 425 sq. ft.
Bedrooms: 4
Bathrooms: 4 ½
Width: 81' - 6"
Depth: 61' - 6"
Foundation: Finished
Walkout Basement
Price Code: L2

Order online @ eplans.com

First Floor

Second Floor

The arrangement of rooms inside this exquisite estate is well-suited for a variety of lifestyles. The dining room and great room provide the opportunity for formal receiving and entertaining. For casual living, look to the spacious kitchen, breakfast room, or keeping room with its welcoming fireplace. Convenient yet private, the master suite is designed to take full advantage of the adjacent study and family area. The second floor contains three bedrooms, three full baths, and a bonus room that also functions as Bedroom 5.

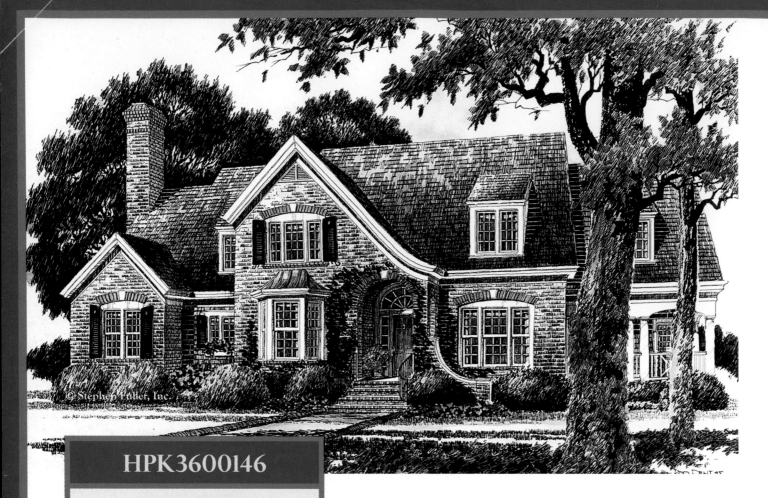

© Stephen Fuller, Inc.

HPK3600146

First Floor: 2,526 sq. ft.
Second Floor: 1,720 sq. ft.
Total: 4,246 sq. ft.
Bedrooms: 4
Bathrooms: 3 ½
Width: 77' - 6"
Depth: 62' - 0"
Foundation: Crawlspace
Price Code: L2

Order online @ eplans.com

CORDOVA PLACE

First Floor

Second Floor

This English country home puts its best face forward. Locating the garage in a rear corner makes room for plenty of charming details up front: an enchanting arched entry, a tiny walled garden, and a side porch. Inside, multiple fireplaces and beamed ceilings enhance the country feeling. A great home for families with children, this design features three family bedrooms in addition to the master suite, an open flex area on the second floor, and a quiet space outfitted for a computer or two.

© Stephen Fuller, Inc.

HPK3600147

First Floor: 3,365 sq. ft.
Second Floor: 1,456 sq. ft.
Total: 4,821 sq. ft.
Bonus Space: 341 sq. ft.
Bedrooms: 4
Bathrooms: 3 ½
Width: 81' - 0"
Depth: 71' - 9"
Foundation: Finished
Walkout Basement
Price Code: L2

Order online @ eplans.com

OXFORD HALL

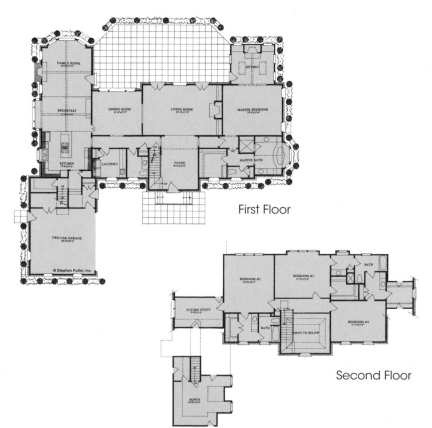

© Stephen Fuller, Inc.

First Floor

Second Floor

The lines of this formal Georgian brick manor are graceful and flowing. The inviting two-story foyer is highlighted by its view through the living room to the large patio. The tasteful entertaining area of the home is complemented by the spacious living area which includes the kitchen, the breakfast room, and the family room. Upstairs are three large bedrooms with baths.

© Stephen Fuller, Inc.

HPK3600148

First Floor: 3,509 sq. ft.
Second Floor: 1,564 sq. ft.
Total: 5,073 sq. ft.
Bedrooms: 4
Bathrooms: 4½ + ½
Width: 86' - 6"
Depth: 67' - 3"
Foundation: Finished
Walkout Basement
Price Code: L2

Order online @ eplans.com

BUCKINGHAM COURT

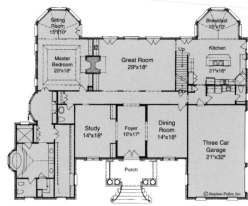

First Floor

Symmetry combined with classical detailing proclaims this estate as the very finest in elegant architecture. Designed on the traditional center-hall principle, the home sustains both grand formal spaces and intimate casual areas. The study connects to the master suite, but is also accessible from the foyer, making it a fine home office. The master suite spotlights a tray ceiling, a huge walk-in closet, and a resplendent bath.

Second Floor

452 MANDERLEIGH

HPK3600149

First Floor: 3,703 sq. ft.
Second Floor: 1,427 sq. ft.
Total: 5,130 sq. ft.
Bonus Space: 1,399 sq. ft.
Bedrooms: 4
Bathrooms: 3½ + ½
Width: 125' - 2"
Depth: 58' - 10"
Foundation: Finished
Walkout Basement
Price Code: L2

Order online @ eplans.com

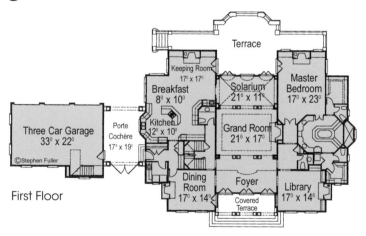

First Floor

Terrace

Keeping Room
17⁰ x 17⁰

Breakfast
8⁰ x 10⁰

Solarium
21⁶ x 11⁰

Master Bedroom
17⁰ x 23⁰

Three Car Garage
33⁰ x 22⁰

Porte Cochère
17³ x 19⁰

©Stephen Fuller

Kitchen
12⁰ x 10⁰

Grand Room
21⁶ x 17⁰

Dining Room
17⁰ x 14⁰

Foyer

Library
17⁰ x 14⁶

Covered Terrace

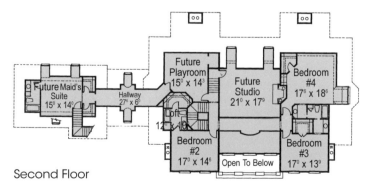

Second Floor

Future Maid's Suite
15⁰ x 14⁰

Hallway
27⁰ x 6⁰

Future Playroom
15⁰ x 14³

Future Studio
21⁰ x 17⁹

Bedroom #4
17⁶ x 18⁶

Loft
12⁰ x 10⁰

Bedroom #2
17⁰ x 14⁶

Open To Below

Bedroom #3
17⁰ x 13⁹

This magnificent estate is detailed with exterior charm: a porte cochere connecting the detached garage to the house, a covered terrace, and oval windows. The first floor consists of a lavish master suite, a library with a fireplace, a grand room/solarium combination, a formal dining room with another fireplace, and a kitchen/breakfast room/keeping room that will delight everyone in the family. Three large bedrooms dominate the second level, each with a walk-in closet.

© Stephen Fuller, Inc.

HPK3600150

First Floor: 3,773 sq. ft.
Second Floor: 1,361 sq. ft.
Bedrooms: 5
Bathrooms: 5 ½
Width: 78' - 3"
Depth: 104' - 3"
Foundation: Unfinished Basement
Price Code: SQ7

Order online @ eplans.com

PEMBROKE HALL

Locating the three-car garage at the rear of the home allows the classic Georgian facade of this elegant manor to shine. A modified center-hall plan puts the study to one side of the foyer and the dining room to the other. Beyond the open stairway, however, the plan opens up to a generously-sized family room. Venture to the keeping room on the other side of the kitchen for even more comfortable space.

First Floor

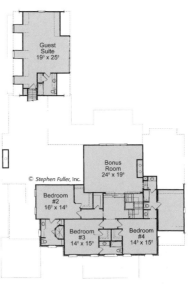

Second Floor

© Stephen Fuller, Inc.

BOURGOGNE

First Floor

Second Floor

HPK3600151

First Floor: 2,864 sq. ft.
Second Floor: 2,329 sq. ft.
Total: 5,193 sq. ft.
Bedrooms: 4
Bathrooms: 4½ + ½
Width: 64' - 6"
Depth: 87' - 6"
Foundation: Unfinished
Walkout Basement
Price Code: L2

Order online @ eplans.com

At nearly 5,200 square feet, this French Country beauty is replete with luxurious amenities inside that match the elegance outside. Formal living spaces are made contemporary with upgraded ceiling treatments and abundant space. The expansive great room is ideal for social gatherings with convenient access to the rear back porch. To the left, the first-floor master bedroom provides privacy and seclusion. Upstairs, the three family bedrooms each boast a full bath. Friends and family alike will indulge in the ever popular media room.

HPK3600152

First Floor: 3,568 sq. ft.
Second Floor: 1,667 sq. ft.
Total: 5,235 sq. ft.
Bedrooms: 4
Bathrooms: 3 ½
Width: 86' - 8"
Depth: 79' - 0"
Foundation: Finished
Walkout Basement
Price Code: L2

Order online @ eplans.com

ROSEWOOD VILLA

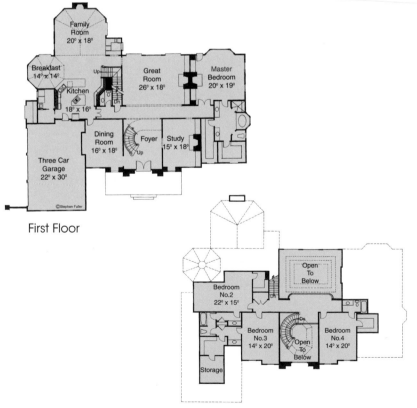

First Floor

Second Floor

Ornamental stucco on the facade of this home creates Old World charm. The foyer, with a curved stair, opens to the dining room, study, and two-story great room. A kitchen with an island workstation adjoins an octagonal breakfast room and the family room. Convenient access to the study, a fireplace, two walk-in closets, and a bath with twin vanities and a separate shower and tub comprise the master suite. A staircase off the family room provides additional access to the three second-floor bedrooms.

AZALEA HALL

HPK3600153

First Floor: 3,669 sq. ft.
Second Floor: 2,145 sq. ft.
Total: 5,814 sq. ft.
Bonus Space: 756 sq. ft.
Bedrooms: 4
Bathrooms: 4½ + ½
Width: 85' - 0"
Depth: 95' - 0"
Foundation: Unfinished Walkout Basement
Price Code: SQ3

Order online @ eplans.com

First Floor

Second Floor

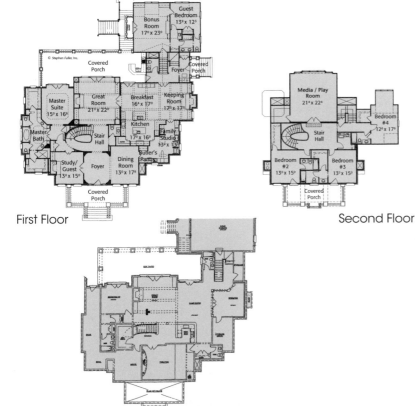

This neoclassical home features exquisite proportions paired with refined details. The foyer is flanked by the study and dining room. The great room has a warming fireplace and access to the rear covered porch. The breakfast room, keeping room, and kitchen are all open and feature coffered ceilings. A guest suite with bonus room can be entered through a rear foyer. The master suite and luxurious bath are at the left side of the plan. The second floor features three bedrooms with private baths and a media room.

© Stephen Fuller, Inc.

HPK3600154

First Floor: 3,902 sq. ft.
Second Floor: 2,159 sq. ft.
Total: 6,061 sq. ft.
Bedrooms: 5
Bathrooms: 3 ½
Width: 85' - 3"
Depth: 74' - 0"
Foundation: Finished
Walkout Basement
Price Code: L2

Order online @ eplans.com

180 BRIDGEPORT PLANT

First Floor

Second Floor

The entry to this classic home is framed with a sweeping double staircase and four large columns topped with a pediment. The two-story foyer is flanked by spacious living and dining rooms. The two-story family room, which has a central fireplace, opens to the study and a solarium. A spacious U-shaped kitchen features a central island cooktop. An additional staircase off the breakfast room offers convenient access to the second floor. The impressive master suite features backyard access and a bath fit for royalty.

© Stephen Fuller, Inc.

CUMBERLAND RIVER COTTAGE

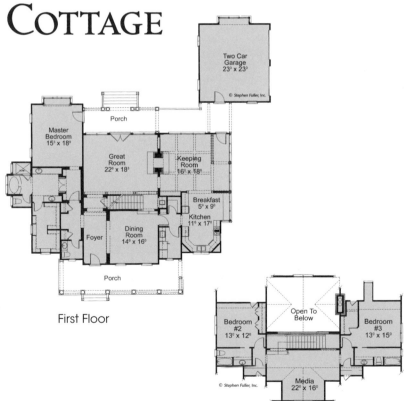

Two Car Garage
23³ x 23³

© Stephen Fuller, Inc.

Porch

Master Bedroom
15³ x 18⁰

Great Room
22⁶ x 18³

Keeping Room
16² x 18⁸

Breakfast
5⁰ x 9⁰

Foyer

Dining Room
14⁰ x 16⁰

Kitchen
11⁸ x 17⁰

Porch

First Floor

Open To Below

Bedroom #2
13⁰ x 12⁶

Bedroom #3
13⁰ x 15⁰

© Stephen Fuller, Inc.

Media
22⁰ x 16⁰

Second Floor

HPK3600155

First Floor: 2,565 sq. ft.
Second Floor: 1,075 sq. ft.
Total: 3,640 sq. ft.
Bedrooms: 3
Bathrooms: 3 ½
Width: 68' - 3"
Depth: 31' - 3"
Foundation: Unfinished Walkout Basement
Price Code: L1

Order online @ eplans.com

A wide and welcoming front porch topped by a balustrade gives this modest home a sense of grandeur. Inside, brilliant planning makes the most of every square foot. Rooms for entertaining flow gracefully into intimate spaces; the great room is linked to the less-formal keeping room by a great stone fireplace. The master suite is sequestered to the left of the plan, but still enjoys access to the rear porch. Upstairs, two private bedroom suites open to a common area.

© Stephen Fuller, Inc.

HPK3600156

First Floor: 2,502 sq. ft.
Second Floor: 1,228 sq. ft.
Total: 3,730 sq. ft.
Bedrooms: 4
Bathrooms: 3 ½
Width: 78' - 9"
Depth: 71' - 9"
Foundation: Unfinished
Walkout Basement
Price Code: L1

Order online @ eplans.com

YORKSHIRE

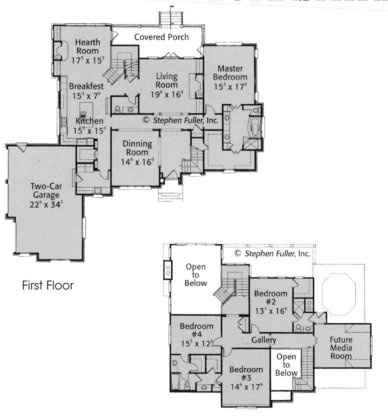

First Floor

Second Floor

The craftsmanship of this Tudor-style home's English ancestors prevails with half-timbered construction. These wooden accents, along with brick and stone, create a gracious, timeless appeal. Inside, an open floor plan is perfect for entertaining. The kitchen is just as functional as it is pretty. It features ample storage and workspace. Upstairs three secondary bedrooms and two bathrooms complete the space. The bonus room over the three-car garage is perfect for a media or scrapbooking room.

© Stephen Fuller, Inc.

KENNESAW RIDGE

To Detached Garage

Master Bedroom
18³ x 18⁹

Porch

Keeping Room
11⁰ x 8⁸

© Stephen Fuller, Inc.

Family Room
20³ x 22³

Breakfast
14⁰ x 14⁹

Kitchen
12⁰ x 16⁸

Foyer

Living Room
15⁰ x 18⁰

Dining Room
12³ x 16⁰

Porch

First Floor

© Stephen Fuller, Inc.

Vaulted Family Room Below

Bedroom #4
12⁰ x 14³

Bedroom #3
12⁸ x 10⁰

Bedroom #2
15³ x 18⁰

Second Floor

HPK3600157

First Floor: 2,909 sq. ft.
Second Floor: 1,042 sq. ft.
Total: 3,951 sq. ft.
Bedrooms: 4
Bathrooms: 3 ½
Width: 71' - 0"
Depth: 65' - 0"
Foundation: Unfinished Walkout Basement
Price Code: L1

Order online @ eplans.com

This two-story cottage exudes southern charm. The foyer leads to a living room and family room, where vaulted ceilings make the area feel even more spacious. The breakfast nook is adjacent to the kitchen, as is a keeping room. The master suite, with private bath and walk-in closet, is also on the main level. Three bedrooms on the upstairs provide additional sleeping quarters. A wraparound porch is accessible from the central hallway, breakfast area, and master bedroom, and leads to the detached garage.

© Stephen Fuller, Inc.

HPK3600158

First Floor: 2,958 sq. ft.
Second Floor: 1,457 sq. ft.
Total: 4,415 sq. ft.
Bedrooms: 4
Bathrooms: 5 ½
Width: 59' - 3"
Depth: 81' - 9"
Foundation: Unfinished Basement
Price Code: L1

Order online @ eplans.com

LEYLAND PLACE

This handsome Tudor bungalow is perfect for a narrow lot. The plan revolves around the beam-ceilinged great room, which is dominated by a fireplace flanked by built-in cabinetry. A butler's pantry leads to the columned dining room, which opens through French doors to the entry terrace. The left side of the plan houses the master suite, where a bay-shaped wall of windows impresses. An L-shaped stair rises through a radial opening to the second floor, which features three generous bedrooms, each with its own private baths and walk-in closet.

First Floor

Second Floor

© Stephen Fuller, Inc.

BLYTHEWOOD

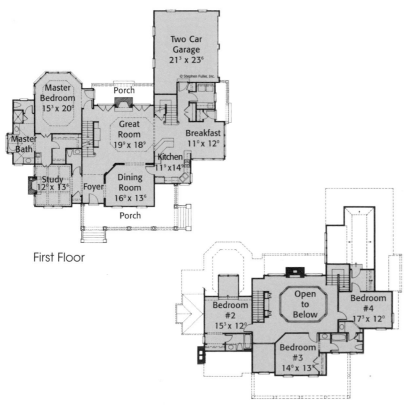

First Floor

- Two Car Garage 21³ x 23⁶
- © Stephen Fuller, Inc.
- Master Bedroom 15³ x 20⁰
- Porch
- Master Bath
- Great Room 19⁹ x 18⁹
- Breakfast 11⁰ x 12⁰
- Kitchen 11⁹ x 14⁹
- Study 12⁰ x 13⁶
- Foyer
- Dining Room 16⁰ x 13⁶
- Porch

Second Floor

- Bedroom #2 15³ x 12⁹
- Open to Below
- Bedroom #4 17³ x 12⁰
- Bedroom #3 14⁰ x 13⁰

HPK3600159

First Floor: 2,332 sq. ft.
Second Floor: 1,836 sq. ft.
Total: 4,168 sq. ft.
Bedrooms: 4
Bathrooms: 3 ½
Width: 73' - 0"
Depth: 72' - 0"
Foundation: Unfinished Walkout Basement
Price Code: L1

Order online @ eplans.com

Classic details and timeless charm says it all. This four-bedroom beauty inspires admiration in any neighborhood. The roomy front porch is immediately appealing. Inside, towering ceilings distinguish the great room. Private access from the master suite to the study invites a cozy evening of fireside reading. The layout of the kitchen, breakfast, and dining room is convenient and efficient. Two staircases access the second floor, where there are three secondary bedrooms, one private full bath, and a Jack-and-Jill bath.

Rear Exterior

HPK3600160

First Floor: 3,132 sq. ft.
Second Floor: 2,280 sq. ft.
Total: 5,412 sq. ft.
Bedrooms: 4
Bathrooms: 3 ½
Width: 99' - 3"
Depth: 93' - 6"
Foundation: Unfinished Basement
Price Code: L2

Order online @ eplans.com

MEADOWVIEW

Brimming with curb appeal, this modern Colonial boasts spacious common areas and lavish sleeping quarters. Three fireplaces on the first floor add ambiance and warmth. The porte cochere offers a convenient entrance for guests despite the weather. On the second floor, three secondary bedrooms share two full baths. A bonus room above the garage is great for guests or a teenager. The size of the game room invites the possibility of a pool table.

First Floor

Second Floor

Rear Exterior

WOODMONT

First Floor

- One Car Garage 13x22
- Keeping Room 15⁰x17⁹
- Kitchen 15⁶x14³
- Breakfast 15⁶x13⁶
- Deck
- Great Room 18⁶x19⁶
- Master Bedroom 15⁶x14⁶
- Master Bath
- Dining Room 13⁰x15⁶
- Foyer
- Two Car Garage 23⁶x24
- Porch
- © Stephen Fuller, Inc.

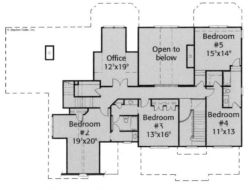

Second Floor

- Office 12⁵x19⁹
- Open to below
- Bedroom #5 15⁵x14⁶
- Bedroom #2 19⁵x20⁶
- Bedroom #3 13⁰x16⁰
- Bedroom #4 11³x13
- © Stephen Fuller, Inc.

HPK3600161

First Floor: 2,628 sq. ft.
Second Floor: 1,775 sq. ft.
Total: 4,403 sq. ft.
Bedrooms: 5
Bathrooms: 3 ½
Width: 79' - 6"
Depth: 65' - 1"
Foundation: Unfinished Walkout Basement
Price Code: L2

Order online @ eplans.com

With five bedrooms and a wonderful stone-and-siding exterior, this country home will satisfy every need. Two sets of French doors provide access to the dining room and foyer. The great room enjoys a warming fireplace and deck access. A charming sitting room in a bay window sets off the master bedroom. Four bedrooms, an office, and two full baths complete the upper level.

HPK3600162

First Floor: 2,161 sq. ft.
Second Floor: 2,110 sq. ft.
Total: 4,271 sq. ft.
Bedrooms: 4
Bathrooms: 3 ½
Width: 76' - 2"
Depth: 60' - 11"
Foundation: Finished
Walkout Basement
Price Code: L2

Order online @ eplans.com

Stucco and stone create charm in this French Country estate. The living and dining rooms flank the foyer, creating a functional formal area. The den or family room is positioned at the rear of the home with convenient access to the kitchen, patio, and covered arbor. A large butler's pantry is located near the kitchen and dining room. Upstairs, the vaulted master suite and three large bedrooms provide private retreats.

ASHLAND GROVE

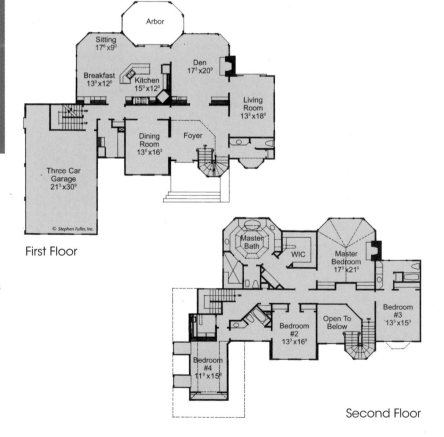

First Floor

Second Floor

© Stephen Fuller, Inc.

HPK3600163

First Floor: 2,346 sq. ft.
Second Floor: 1,260 sq. ft.
Total: 3,606 sq. ft.
Bedrooms: 4
Bathrooms: 3 ½
Width: 68' - 11"
Depth: 58' - 9"
Foundation: Finished
Walkout Basement
Price Code: L1

Order online @ eplans.com

HAMSTEAD FARM

First Floor

Second Floor

The European character of this home is enhanced through the use of stucco and stone. The foyer leads to the dining room and study/living room. The family room is positioned for convenient access to the back staircase, kitchen, wet bar, and deck. The master bedroom is privately located on the right side of the home, with an optional entry to the study and a large garden bath. Upstairs are three additional bedrooms.

© Stephen Fuller, Inc.

HPK3600164

First Floor: 2,871 sq. ft.
Second Floor: 1,407 sq. ft.
Total: 4,278 sq. ft.
Bonus Space: 324 sq. ft.
Bedrooms: 4
Bathrooms: 4 ½
Width: 89' - 3"
Depth: 60' - 10"
Foundation: Finished
Walkout Basement
Price Code: L2

Order online @ eplans.com

RALEIGH COURT

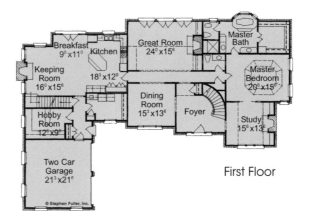

First Floor

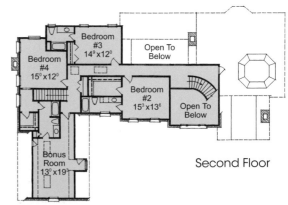

Second Floor

Brick details, casement windows, and large expanses of glass add an Old World touch of glamour to this two-story home. Sunlight streams in the two-story foyer, which is highlighted by a sweeping balustrade. For formal occasions, look to the spacious dining room, inviting study, and vaulted great room. The kitchen, breakfast room, and keeping room are for casual family living. The quiet master suite has a sumptuous bath and access to the study through pocket doors. Upstairs, three secondary bedrooms each have private baths.

© Stephen Fuller, Inc

CLAIRMONT MANOR

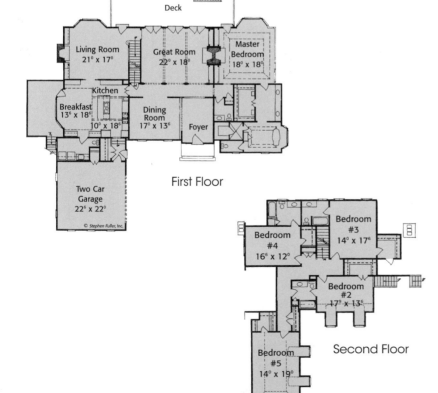

First Floor

- Deck
- Living Room 21⁰ x 17⁰
- Great Room 22⁰ x 18⁰
- Master Bedroom 18⁰ x 18⁰
- Kitchen
- Breakfast 13⁶ x 18⁶
- 10⁰ x 18⁶
- Dining Room 17⁰ x 13⁶
- Foyer
- Two Car Garage 22⁶ x 22⁰

© Stephen Fuller, Inc.

Second Floor

- Bedroom #4 16⁶ x 12⁰
- Bedroom #3 14⁰ x 17⁶
- Bedroom #2 17⁰ x 13⁶
- Bedroom #5 14⁰ x 19⁰

HPK3600165

First Floor: 2,929 sq. ft.
Second Floor: 1,624 sq. ft.
Total: 4,553 sq. ft.
Bedrooms: 5
Bathrooms: 4½ + ½
Width: 75' - 11"
Depth: 69' - 0"
Foundation: Finished Walkout Basement
Price Code: L2

Order online @ eplans.com

Textured stucco blends with ornate details and a steep hipped roof to create a historic-style home. Columns announce the vaulted great room, flooded with light from triple French doors. In the nearby living room, a fireplace warms and a bay window makes a cozy reading nook. Enjoy a gourmet experience with every meal in the well-appointed kitchen. The master suite is romantic, with a fireplace, bay, and spa bath. On the upper level, two suites have private baths; two dormered bedrooms share a full bath.

© Stephen Fuller, Inc.

HPK3600166

First Floor: 2,452 sq. ft.
Second Floor: 1,309 sq. ft.
Total: 3,761 sq. ft.
Bonus Space: 240 sq. ft.
Bedrooms: 4
Bathrooms: 3½ + ½
Width: 59' - 6"
Depth: 81' - 0"
Foundation: Unfinished
Walkout Basement
Price Code: L1

Order online @ eplans.com

COUNTRY CHICKERING

Corner boards, cornice, and other exterior moldings enhance the country retreat look, while the light, bright interiors meet the needs of a variety of lifestyles. Inside, rooms are arranged around the foyer and its central staircase. Downstairs living areas flow from the family room through the breakfast area and kitchen into the dining room, study, and master suite. Upstairs, the staircase and gallery overlook serve to separate the three bedrooms.

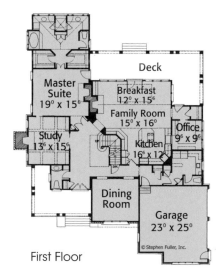

First Floor

Deck

Master Suite 19⁰ x 15⁶

Breakfast 12⁰ x 15⁶

Family Room 15⁰ x 16⁰

Office 9⁶ x 9⁶

Study 13⁶ x 15⁶

Kitchen 16⁶ x 12⁶

Dining Room

Garage 23⁰ x 25⁰

© Stephen Fuller, Inc.

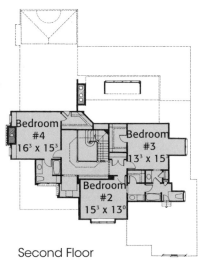

Second Floor

Bedroom #4 16³ x 15³

Bedroom #3 13³ x 15

Bedroom #2 15³ x 13⁰

© Stephen Fuller, Inc.

MILLSTEAD

Two Car Garage
22⁶ x 21³

© Stephen Fuller, Inc.

Porch

Deck

UP

Living Room
20³ x 15³

Master Bedroom
14³ x 15³

Family Room
12³ x 21⁰

Kitchen
13⁰ x 17⁶

© Stephen Fuller, Inc.

Dining Room
12³ x 13⁹

Study
13³ x 11⁹

Porch

First Floor

Bedroom #4
11³ x 21³

DN

© Stephen Fuller, Inc.

Study Nook

Bedroom #3
15⁹ x 11⁶

Attic Stor.

Bedroom #2
12³ x 15⁰

Second Floor

HPK3600167

First Floor: 2,362 sq. ft.
Second Floor: 1,350 sq. ft.
Total: 3,712 sq. ft.
Bedrooms: 4
Bathrooms: 3 ½
Width: 77' - 3"
Depth: 56' - 3"
Foundation: Unfinished Walkout Basement
Price Code: L1

Order online @ eplans.com

Natural materials and a wide footprint blend this home with the surrounding landscape. Inside, the vista is wide open, as walls are replaced by columns to delineate the formal rooms. Family rooms are separated to the right of the plan in an open layout, and the master suite lies to the left for maximum privacy. The corner fireplace here is mirrored by one in the living room. A third fireplace occupies the family room.

Dreaming is free. And now, so are shipping & handling.

At Eplans, we know one of the best things about dreaming up even the most luxurious home is that it doesn't cost you a cent. And while we can't help with the expense of building your project, for a limited time we can cut the cost of finding the perfect plan by giving you free shipping on up to 8 of our outstanding home plan books you order. So stock up, because right now shipping and handling on home idea books are as free as dreaming about them.

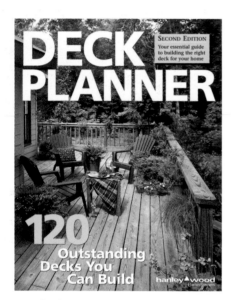

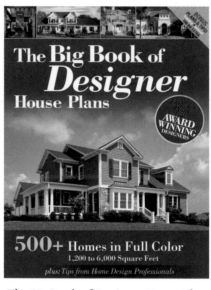

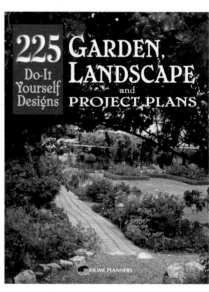

Deck Planner
From broad and expansive to small and intimate, you'll find plans in every shape and size, plus basic deck-building information, to create the perfect outdoor space for entertaining, relaxing and recreation. 144 pages—32 full color.
Code: DP2 $9.95

The Big Book of Designer House Plans
Full-color photographs, renderings and detailed descriptions bring hundreds of architectural gems ranging from 1,999sq. ft. Starter Homes to 4,000+ sq. ft. Luxury Manors to vivid life. 464 full-color pages.
Code: HPK29 $12.95

Garden Landscape and Project Plans
Let your imagination take flight with plans for butterfly gardens, workshops, porch swings, landscape plans and more with everything you need to transform an ordinary yard into an extraordinary outdoor show place. 320 full-color pages.
Code: GLP $19.95

350 Two-Story Home Plans
Fresh ideas for inside and out. The nation's top designers make these two stories terrific.
Code: HPK27 $12.95

Waterfront Homes
Imagine the possibilities with 200 view-maximizing home plans tailor-made for life on the river, lake or sea.
Code: WF2 $10.95

European Elegance
Explore more than 100 modern-day home designs featuring the architectural heritages of France, Italy, Spain and England.
Code: HPK22 $19.95

Victorian
Relive the historic elegance of Victorian times with 165 new house plans that bring back the romance of front porches, turrets, and gingerbread trim.
Code: HPK28 $10.95

Call toll-free 1-800-322-6797

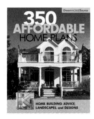

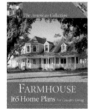

With more than 50 years of experience in the industry and millions of blueprints sold, Hanley Wood is a trusted source of high-quality, high-value pre-drawn home plans.

Using pre-drawn home plans is a **reliable, cost-effective way** to build your dream home, and our vast selection of plans is second-to-none. The nation's finest designers craft these plans that builders know they can trust. Meanwhile, our friendly, knowledgeable customer service representatives can help you every step of the way.

WHAT YOU'LL GET WITH YOUR ORDER

The contents of each designer's blueprint package is unique, but all contain detailed, high-quality working drawings. You can expect to find the following standard elements in most sets of plans:

I. FRONT PERSPECTIVE

This artist's sketch of the exterior of the house gives you an idea of how the house will look when built and landscaped.

2. FOUNDATION AND BASE-MENT PLANS

This sheet shows the foundation layout including concrete walls, footings, pads, posts, beams, bearing walls, and foundation notes. If the home features a basement, the first-floor framing details may also be included on this plan. If your plan features slab construction rather than a basement, the plan shows footings and details for a monolithic slab. This page, or another in the set, may include a sample plot plan for locating your house on a building site. Additional sheets focus on foundation cross-sections and other details.

3. DETAILED FLOOR PLANS

These plans show the layout of each floor of the house. Rooms and interior spaces are carefully dimensioned, doors and windows located, and keys are given for cross-section details provided elsewhere in the plans.

4. HOUSE AND DETAIL CROSS-SECTIONS

Large-scale views show sections or cutaways of the foundation, interior walls, exterior walls, floors, stairways, and roof details. Additional cross-sections may show important changes in floor, ceiling, or roof heights, or the relationship of one level to another. These sections show exactly how the various parts of the house fit together and are extremely valuable during construction. Additional sheets may include enlarged wall, floor, and roof construction details.

5. FLOOR STRUCTURAL SUPPORTS

The floor framing plans provide detail for these crucial elements of your home. Each includes floor joist, ceiling joist, spacing, direction, span, and specifications. Beam and window headers, along with necessary details for framing connections, stairways, or dormers are also included.

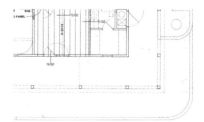

6. ELECTRICAL PLAN

The electrical plan offers suggested locations with notes for all lighting, outlets, switches, and circuits. A layout is provided for each level, as well as basements, garages, or other structures. This plan does not contain diagrams detailing how all wiring should be run, or how circuits should be engineered. These details should be designed by your electrician.

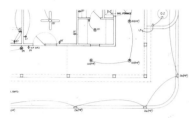

7. EXTERIOR ELEVATIONS

In addition to the front exterior, your blueprint set will include drawings of the rear and sides of your house as well. These drawings give notes on exterior materials and finishes. Particular attention is given to cornice detail, brick and stone accents, or other finish items that make your home unique.

ROOF FRAMING PLANS— PLEASE READ

Some plans contain roof framing plans; however because of the wide variation in local requirements, many plans do not. If you buy a plan without a roof framing plan, you will need an engineer familiar with local building codes to create a plan to build your roof. Even if your plan does contain a roof framing plan, we recommend that a local engineer review the plan to verify that it will meet local codes.

BEFORE YOU CALL

You are making a terrific decision to use a pre-drawn house plan—it is one you can make with confidence, knowing that your blueprints are crafted by national-award-winning certified residential designers and architects, and trusted by builders.

Once you've selected the plan you want—or even if you have questions along the way—our experienced customer service representatives are available to help you navigate the home-building process. To help them provide you with even better service, please consider the following questions before you call:

■ Have you chosen or purchased your lot?
If so, please review the building setback requirements of your local building authority before you call. You don't need to have a lot before ordering plans, but if you own land already, please have the width and depth dimensions handy when you call.

■ Have you chosen a builder?
Involving your builder in the plan selection and evaluation process may be beneficial. Luckily, builders know they can have confidence with pre-drawn plans because they've been designed for livability, functionality, and typically are builder-proven at successful home sites across the country.

■ Do you need a construction loan?
Construction loans are unique because they involve determining the value of something that is not yet constructed. Several lenders offer convenient contstruction-to-permanent loans. It is important to choose a good lending partner—one who will help guide you through the application and appraisal process. Most will even help you evaluate your contractor to ensure reliability and credit worthiness. Our partnership with IndyMac Bank, a nationwide leader in construction loans, can help you save on your loan, if needed.

■ How many sets of plans do you need?
Building a home can typically require a number of sets of blueprints—one for yourself, two or three for the builder and subcontractors, two for the local building department, and one or more for your lender. For this reason, we offer 5-, 8-, and Reproducible plan packages, but your best value is the CAD Package, which includes a copy of the digital file used to create the home

design. By using CAD software, it is easy to print hard copies of blueprints. Reproducible plans are tremendously flexible in that they allow you to make up to 12 duplicates of the plan so you have enough copies of the plan for everyone involved in the financing and construction of your home.

■ Do you want to make any changes to the plan?
We understand that it is difficult to find blueprints for a home that will meet all of your needs. That is why Hanley Wood is glad to offer plan Customization Services. We will work with you to design the modifications you'd like to see and to adjust your blueprint plans accordingly—anything from changing the foundation; adding square footage, redesigning baths, kitchens, or bedrooms; or most other modifications. This simple, cost-effective service saves you from hiring an outside architect to make alterations. Modifications may only be made to Reproducible or CAD Plan Packages that include the license to modify. Purchasing a CAD file may save you money if you intend to make changes, because CAD files can be directly modified.

■ Do you have to make any changes to meet local building codes?
While all of our plans are drawn to meet national building codes at the time they were created, many areas required that plans be stamped by a local engineer to certify that they meet local building codes. Building codes are updated frequently and can vary by state, county, city, or municipality. Contact your local building inspection department, office of planning and zoning, or department of permits to determine how your local codes will affect your construction project. The best way to assure that you can make changes to your plan, if necessary, is to purchase a Reproducible or CAD Plan Package.

■ Has everyone—from family members to contractors—been involved in selecting the plan?
Building a new home is an exciting process, and using pre-drawn plans is a great way to realize your dreams. Make sure that everyone involved has had an opportunity to review the plan you've selected. While Hanley Wood does have an exchange policy, it's best to be sure all parties agree on your selection before you buy.

CALL TOLL-FREE 1–800–521–6797

Source Key
HPK36

CUSTOMIZE YOUR PLAN – HANLEY WOOD CUSTOMIZATION SERVICES

Creating custom home plans has never been easier and more directly accessible. Using state-of-the-art technology and top-performing architectural expertise, Hanley Wood delivers on a long-standing customer commitment to provide world-class home-plans and customization services. Our valued customers—professional home builders and individual home owners—appreciate the convenience and accessibility of this interactive, consultative service.

With the Hanley Wood Customization Service you can:
- Save valuable time by avoiding drawn-out and frequently repetitive face-to-face design meetings
- Communicate design and home-plan changes faster and more efficiently
- Speed-up project turn-around time
- Build on a budget without sacrificing quality
- Transform master home plans to suit your design needs and unique personal style

All of our design options and prices are impressively affordable. A detailed quote is available for a $50 consultation fee. Plan modification is an interactive service. Our skilled team of designers will guide you through the customization process from start to finish making recommendations, offering ideas, and determining the feasibility of your changes. This level of service is offered to ensure the final modified plan meets your expectations. If you use our service the $50 fee will be applied to the cost of the modifications.

You may purchase the customization consultation before or after purchasing a plan. In either case, it is necessary to purchase the Reproducible or CAD Plan Package and complete the accompanying license to modify the plan before we can begin customization.

Customization Estimate and Consultation. $50

TOOLS TO WORK WITH YOUR BUILDER

Two Reverse Options For Your Convenience – Mirror and Right-Reading Reverse (as available)

Mirror reverse plans simply flip the design 180 degrees—keep in mind, the text will also be flipped. For a minimal fee you can have one or all of your plans shipped mirror reverse, although we recommend having at least one regular set handy. Right-reading reverse plans show the design flipped 180 degrees but the text reads normally. When you choose this option, we ship each set of purchased blueprints in this format.

Mirror Reverse Fee (indicate the number of sets when ordering) $55

Right Reading Reverse Fee (all sets are reversed). $175

Know Before You Build – Cost-to-Build Calculator

Ultimate Cost-to-Build Calculator helps you quickly and easily discover the answer to the number-one question in construction: How much will it cost to build this house? This remarkable online tool allows you to personalize the cost-to-build schedule for any home plan you choose. Experiment with different material choices and change home features with a few clicks, and compare prices. All estimates are specific to your home plan and geographic region.

The Ultimate Cost-to-Build Calculator $29.95

A Shopping List Exclusively for Your Home – Materials List

A customized Materials List helps you plan and estimate the cost of your new home, outlining the quantity, type, and size of materials needed to build your house (with the exception of mechanical system items). Included are framing lumber, windows and doors, kitchen and bath cabinetry, rough and finished hardware, and much more.

Materials List. . . . . $85 – $150 each

Additional Materials Lists (at original time of purchase only). . .$20 each

Plan Your Home-Building Process – Specification Outline

Work with your builder on this step-by-step chronicle of 166 stages or items crucial to the building process. It provides a comprehensive review of the construction process and helps you choose materials.

Specification Outline . . . .$10 each

Learn the Basics of Building – Electrical, Plumbing, Mechanical, Construction Detail Sheets

If you want to know more about building techniques—and deal more confidently with your subcontractors—we offer four useful detail sheets. These sheets provide non-plan-specific general information, but are excellent tools that will add to your understanding of Plumbing Details, Electrical Details, Construction Details, and Mechanical Details.

Electrical Detail Sheet $14.95

Plumbing Detail Sheet. $14.95

Mechanical Detail Sheet $14.95

Construction Detail Sheet. $14.95

SUPER VALUE SETS:
Buy any 2: $26.95; Buy any 3: $34.95; Buy All 4: $39.95

Best Value

MAKE YOUR HOME TECH-READY – HOME AUTOMATION UPGRADE

Building a new home provides a unique opportunity to wire it with a plan for future needs. A Home Automation-Ready (HA-Ready) home contains the wiring substructure of tomorrow's connected home. It means that every room—from the front porch to the backyard, and from the attic to the basement—is wired for security, lighting, telecommunications, climate control, home computer networking, whole-house audio, home theater, shade control, video surveillance, entry access control, and yes, video gaming electronic solutions.

Along with the conveniences HA-Ready homes provide, they also have a higher resale value. The Consumer Electronics Association (CEA), in conjunction with the Custom Electronic Design and Installation Association (CEDIA), have developed a TechHome™ Rating system that quantifies the value of HA-Ready homes. The rating system is gaining widespread recognition in the real estate industry.

Developed by CEDIA-certified installers, our Home Automation Upgrade package includes everything you need to work with an installer during the construction of your home. It provides a short explanation of the various subsystems, a wiring floor plan for each level of your home, a detailed materials list with estimated costs, and a list of CEDIA-certified installers in your local area.

Home Automation Upgrade. $250

GET YOUR HOME PLANS PAID FOR!

IndyMac Bank, in partnership with Hanley Wood, will reimburse you up to $750 toward the cost of your home plans simply by financing the construction of your new home with IndyMac Bank Home Construction Lending.

IndyMac's construction and permanent loan is a one-time close loan, meaning that one application—and one set of closing fees—provides all the financing you need.

Apply today at www.indymacbank.com, call toll free at 1-800-847-6138, or ask a Hanley Wood customer service representative for details.

DESIGN YOUR HOME – INTERIOR AND EXTERIOR FINISHING TOUCHES

Be Your Own Interior Designer! – Home Furniture Planner

Effectively plan the space in your home using our Hands-On Home Furniture Planner. It's fun and easy—no more moving heavy pieces of furniture to see how the room will go together. The kit includes reusable peel-and-stick furniture templates that fit on a 12"x18" laminated layout board—enough space to lay out every room in your house.

Home Furniture Planning Kit $15.95

Enjoy the Outdoors! – Deck Plans

Many of our homes have a corresponding deck plan, sold separately, which includes a Deck Plan Frontal Sheet, Deck Framing and Floor Plans, Deck Elevations, and a Deck Materials List. A Standard Deck Details Package, also available, provides all the how-to information necessary for building any deck. Get both the Deck Plan and the Standard Deck Details Package for one low price in our Complete Deck Building Package. See the price tier chart below and call for deck plan availability.

Create a Professionally Designed Landscape – Landscape Plans

Many of our homes have a front-yard Landscape Plan that is complementary in design to the house plan. These comprehensive Landscape Blueprint Packages include a Frontal Sheet, Plan View, Regionalized Plant & Materials List, a sheet on Planting and Maintaining Your Landscape, Zone Maps, and a Plant Size and Description Guide. Each set of blueprints is a full 18" x 24" with clear, complete instructions in easy-to-read type. Our Landscape Plans are available with a Plant & Materials List adapted by horticultural experts to eight regions of the country. Please specify your region when ordering your plan—see region map below. Call for more information about landscape plan availability and applicable regions.

LANDSCAPE & DECK PRICE SCHEDULE

PRICE TIERS	1-SET STUDY PACKAGE	5-SET BUILDING PACKAGE	1-SET REPRODUCIBLE*	1-SET CAD*
P1	$25	$55	$145	$245
P2	$45	$75	$165	$280
P3	$75	$105	$195	$330
P4	$105	$135	$225	$385
P5	$175	$205	$405	$690
P6	$215	$245	$445	$750
D1	$45	$75**	$90	$90
D2	$75	$105**	$150	$150

PRICES SUBJECT TO CHANGE   * REQUIRES AN E-MAIL ADDRESS OR FAX NUMBER
                                  **3-SET BUILDING PACKAGE

TERMS & CONDITIONS

OUR 90-DAY EXCHANGE POLICY

BUY WITH CONFIDENCE!

Hanley Wood is committed to ensuring your satisfaction with your blueprint order, which is why we offer a 90-day exchange policy. With the exception of Reproducible and CAD Plan Package orders, we will exchange your entire first order for an equal or greater number of blueprints from our plan collection within 90 days of the original order. The entire content of your original order must be returned before an exchange will be processed. Please call our customer service department at 1-888-690-1116 for your return authorization number and shipping instructions. If the returned blueprints look used, redlined, or copied, we will not honor your exchange. Fees for exchanging your blueprints are as follows: 20% of the amount of the original order, plus the difference in cost if exchanging for a design in a higher price bracket or less the difference in cost if exchanging for a design in a lower price bracket. (Because they can be copied, Reproducible or CAD blueprints are not exchangeable or refundable.) Please call for current postage and handling prices. Shipping and handling charges are not refundable.

ARCHITECTURAL AND ENGINEERING SEALS

Some cities and states now require that a licensed architect or engineer review and "seal" a blueprint, or officially approve it, prior to construction. Prior to application for a building permit or the start of actual construction, we strongly advise that you consult your local building official who can tell you if such a review is required.

LOCAL BUILDING CODES AND ZONING REQUIREMENTS

Each plan was designed to meet or exceed the requirements of a nationally recognized model building code in effect at the time and place the plan was drawn. Typically plans designed after the year 2000 conform to the International Residential Building Code (IRC 2000 or 2003). The IRC is comprised of portions of the three major codes below. Plans drawn before 2000 conform to one of the three recognized building codes in effect at the time: Building Officials and Code Administrators (BOCA)

CALL TOLL FREE 1-800-521-6797 OR VISIT EPLANS.COM

International, Inc.; the Southern Building Code Congress International, (SBCCI) Inc.; the International Conference of Building Officials (ICBO); or the Council of American Building Officials (CABO).

Because of the great differences in geography and climate throughout the United States and Canada, each state, county, and municipality has its own building codes, zone requirements, ordinances, and building regulations. Your plan may need to be modified to comply with local requirements. In addition, you may need to obtain permits or inspections from local governments before and in the course of construction. We authorize the use of the blueprints on the express condition that you consult a local licensed architect or engineer of your choice prior to beginning construction and strictly comply with all local building codes, zoning requirements, and other applicable laws, regulations, ordinances, and requirements. Notice: Plans for homes to be built in Nevada must be redrawn by a Nevada-registered professional. Consult your local building official for more information on this subject.

TERMS AND CONDITIONS

These designs are protected under the terms of United States Copyright Law and may not be copied or reproduced in any way, by any means, unless you have purchased a Reproducible Plan Package and signed the accompanying license to modify and copy the plan, which clearly indicates your right to modify, copy, or reproduce. We authorize the use of your chosen design as an aid in the construction of ONE (1) single- or multifamily home only. You may not use this design to build a second dwelling or multiple dwellings without purchasing another blueprint or blueprints or paying additional design fees. Multi-use fees vary by designer—please call one of experienced sales representatives for a quote.

DISCLAIMER

The designers we work with have put substantial care and effort into the creation of their blueprints. However, because we cannot provide on-site consultation, supervision, and control over actual construction, and because of the great variance in local building requirements, building practices, and soil, seismic, weather, and other conditions, WE MAKE NO WARRANTY OF ANY KIND, EXPRESS OR IMPLIED, WITH RESPECT TO THE CONTENT OR USE OF THE BLUEPRINTS, INCLUDING BUT NOT LIMITED TO ANY WARRANTY OF MERCHANTABILITY OR OF FITNESS FOR A PARTICULAR PURPOSE. ITEMS, PRICES, TERMS, AND CONDITIONS ARE SUBJECT TO CHANGE WITHOUT NOTICE.

IMPORTANT COPYRIGHT NOTICE
From the Council of Publishing Home Designers

Blueprints for residential construction (or working drawings, as they are often called in the industry) are copyrighted intellectual property, protected under the terms of the United States Copyright Law and, therefore, cannot be copied legally for use in building. The following are some guidelines to help you get what you need to build your home, without violating copyright law:

1. HOME PLANS ARE COPYRIGHTED

Just like books, movies, and songs, home plans receive protection under the federal copyright laws. The copyright laws prevent anyone, other than the copyright owner, from reproducing, modifying, or reusing the plans or design without permission of the copyright owner.

2. DO NOT COPY DESIGNS OR FLOOR PLANS FROM ANY PUBLICATION, ELECTRONIC MEDIA, OR EXISTING HOME

It is illegal to copy, change, or redraw home designs found in a plan book, CDROM or on the Internet. The right to modify plans is one of the exclusive rights of copyright. It is also illegal to copy or redraw a constructed home that is protected by copyright, even if you have never seen the plans for the home. If you find a plan or home that you like, you must purchase a set of plans from an authorized source. The plans may not be lent, given away, or sold by the purchaser.

3. DO NOT USE PLANS TO BUILD MORE THAN ONE HOUSE

The original purchaser of house plans is typically licensed to build a single home from the plans. Building more than one home from the plans without permission is an infringement of the home designer's copyright. The purchase of a multiple-set package of plans is for the construction of a single home only. The purchase of additional sets of plans does not grant the right to construct more than one home.

4. HOUSE PLANS IN THE FORM OF BLUEPRINTS OR BLACKLINES CANNOT BE COPIED OR REPRODUCED

Plans, blueprints, or blacklines, unless they are reproducibles, cannot be copied or reproduced without prior written consent of the copyright owner. Copy shops and blueprinters are prohibited from making copies of these plans without the copyright release letter you receive with reproducible plans.

5. HOUSE PLANS IN THE FORM OF BLUEPRINTS OR BLACKLINES CANNOT BE REDRAWN

Plans cannot be modified or redrawn without first obtaining the copyright owner's permission. With your purchase of plans, you are licensed to make non-structural changes by "red-lining" the purchased plans. If you need to make structural changes or need to redraw the plans for any reason, you must purchase a reproducible set of plans (see topic 6) which includes a license to modify the plans. Blueprints do not come with a license to make structural changes or to redraw the plans. You may not reuse or sell the modified design.

6. REPRODUCIBILE HOME PLANS

Reproducible plans (for example sepias, mylars, CAD files, electronic files, and vellums) come with a license to make modifications to the plans. Once modified, the plans can be taken to a local copy shop or blueprinter to make up to 10 or 12 copies of the plans to use in the construction of a single home. Only one home can be constructed from any single purchased set of reproducible plans either in original form or as modified. The license to modify and copy must be completed and returned before the plan will be shipped.

7. MODIFIED DESIGNS CANNOT BE REUSED

Even if you are licensed to make modifications to a copyrighted design, the modified design is not free from the original designer's copyright. The sale or reuse of the modified design is prohibited. Also, be aware that any modification to plans relieves the original designer from liability for design defects and voids all warranties expressed or implied.

8. WHO IS RESPONSIBLE FOR COPYRIGHT INFRINGEMENT?

Any party who participates in a copyright violation may be responsible including the purchaser, designers, architects, engineers, drafters, homeowners, builders, contractors, sub-contractors, copy shops, blueprinters, developers, and real estate agencies. It does not matter whether or not the individual knows that a violation is being committed. Ignorance of the law is not a valid defense.

9. PLEASE RESPECT HOME DESIGN COPYRIGHTS

In the event of any suspected violation of a copyright, or if there is any uncertainty about the plans purchased, the publisher, architect, designer, or the Council of Publishing Home Designers (www.cphd.org) should be contacted before proceeding. Awards are sometimes offered for information about home design copyright infringement.

10. PENALTIES FOR INFRINGEMENT

Penalties for violating a copyright may be severe. The responsible parties are required to pay actual damages caused by the infringement (which may be substantial), plus any profits made by the infringer commissions to include all profits from the sale of any home built from an infringing design. The copyright law also allows for the recovery of statutory damages, which may be as high as $150,000 for each infringement. Finally, the infringer may be required to pay legal fees which often exceed the damages.

BLUEPRINT PRICE SCHEDULE

PRICE TIERS	1-SET STUDY PACKAGE	5-SET BUILDING PACKAGE	8-SET BUILDING PACKAGE	1-SET REPRODUCIBLE*	1-SET CAD*
A1	$470	$520	$575	$700	$1,055
A2	$510	$565	$620	$765	$1,230
A3	$575	$630	$690	$870	$1,400
A4	$620	$685	$750	$935	$1,570
C1	$665	$740	$810	$1,000	$1,735
C2	$715	$795	$855	$1,065	$1,815
C3	$785	$845	$910	$1,145	$1,915
C4	$840	$915	$970	$1,225	$2,085
L1	$930	$1,030	$1,115	$1,390	$2,500
L2	$1,010	$1,105	$1,195	$1,515	$2,575
L3	$1,115	$1,220	$1,325	$1,665	$2,835
L4	$1,230	$1,350	$1,440	$1,850	$3,140
SQ1				$0.40/SQ. FT.	$0.68/SQ. FT.
SQ3				$0.55/SQ. FT.	$0.94/SQ. FT.
SQ5				$0.80/SQ. FT	$1.36/SQ. FT.
SQ7				$1.00/SQ. FT.	$1.70/SQ. FT.
SQ9				$1.25/SQ. FT.	$2.13/SQ. FT.
SQ11				$1.50/SQ. FT.	$2.55/SQ. FT.

PRICES SUBJECT TO CHANGE

* REQUIRES AN E-MAIL ADDRESS OR FAX NUMBER

PLAN #	PAGE	PLAN NAME	SQUARE FOOTAGE	PRICE TIER	MATERIALS LIST
HPK3600001	6	STEPHENS WALK	2752	C4	
HPK3600002	10	AZALEA HILL	2175	C4	
HPK3600003	11	ACORN HILL	2175	C4	
HPK3600004	12	HILLCREST	2195	C4	
HPK3600005	13	BROOKDALE	2204	C4	
HPK3600006	14	WESTOVER COMMONS	2215	C4	
HPK3600007	15	CARDIFF	2215	C4	
HPK3600008	16	ROE HAMPTON PLACE	2248	C4	
HPK3600009	17	QUINCY HALL	2265	C4	YES
HPK3600010	18	CLANDON	2265	C4	
HPK3600011	19	DAVENPORT COTTAGE	2295	C4	YES
HPK3600012	20	BANFIELD HALL	2325	C4	YES
HPK3600013	21	DUNNING	2325	C4	YES
HPK3600014	22	RICHMOND	2325	C4	
HPK3600015	23	BYRDS RETREAT	2332	C4	
HPK3600016	24	TEN BROECK MANOR	2377	C4	YES
HPK3600017	25	SIERRA	2395	C4	
HPK3600018	26	DOGWOOD WAY	2424	C4	YES
HPK3600019	27	ROCKSPRINGS JUNCTION	2448	C4	
HPK3600020	28	BRADFORD COURT	2482	C4	
HPK3600021	29	COTTONWOOD HOMESTEAD	2485	C4	
HPK3600022	30	PIGEON FALLS	2508	C4	
HPK3600023	31	SALEM FALLS	2515	C4	
HPK3600024	32	SILVER CREEK	2550	C4	
HPK3600025	33	VISALLA	2598	C4	
HPK3600026	34	RIVER FALLS	2665	C4	
HPK3600027	35	ANNIVERSARY COTTAGE	2680	C4	
HPK3600028	36	MAPLE STREET	2706	C4	
HPK3600029	37	HOLLY RIDGE	2710	C4	
HPK3600030	38	THOMASVILLE SHOWHOME	2710	C4	
HPK3600031	39	IVY GLEN	2739	C4	
HPK3600032	40	CHANTERELLE GLEN	2739	C4	
HPK3600033	41	SILVER SPRINGS	2780	C4	

hanley▲wood

PLAN #	PAGE	PLAN NAME	SQUARE FOOTAGE	PRICE TIER	MATERIALS LIST
HPK3600034	42	CHESTNUT LANE	2790	C4	YES
HPK3600035	43	ARBORSHADE	2790	C4	
HPK3600036	44	CAMDEN	2217	C4	
HPK3600037	45	KESWICK	2217	C4	
HPK3600038	46	KENT PARK	2328	C4	
HPK3600039	47	BARKSDALE	2457	C4	YES
HPK3600040	48	CLOVERDALE	2756	C4	
HPK3600041	49	BRISBOIS COURT	1684	C4	YES
HPK3600042	50	WINDERMERE COTTAGE	1695	C4	YES
HPK3600043	51	ELLSWORTH MANOR	1733	C4	YES
HPK3600044	52	HUNTINGTON WAY	1770	L1	YES
HPK3600045	53	ADDISON	1770	C4	
HPK3600046	54	CONCORD	1790	C4	YES
HPK3600047	55	LINTON PARK	1800	C4	
HPK3600048	56	LYNDHURST LODGE	1815	C4	YES
HPK3600049	57	TILLMAN	1815	C4	
HPK3600050	58	YORKTOWN	1850	C4	
HPK3600051	59	CAPE CHARLES PLACE	1939	C4	
HPK3600052	60	WHITEFISH CANYON	2019	C4	
HPK3600053	61	COLBURN COLONIAL	2077	C4	
HPK3600054	62	VAUGHN HOMESTEAD	2077	C4	
HPK3600055	63	JEFFERSON COUNTRY	2090	C4	YES
HPK3600056	64	CANTERBURY RETREAT	2090	C4	YES
HPK3600057	65	STANTON GABLE	2106	C4	YES
HPK3600058	66	STONEMASON PLACE	2120	C4	
HPK3600059	67	TAPPING REEVE RETREAT	2120	C4	YES
HPK3600060	68	SYCAMORE WALK	2150	C4	YES
HPK3600061	69	WOODSIDE WALK	2150	C4	
HPK3600062	70	TYBEE	2170	C4	YES
HPK3600063	71	214 DOGWOOD WAY	2175	C4	YES
HPK3600064	72	SWEETWOOD	3280	L1	
HPK3600065	76	HEDGEWOOD HEIGHTS	3266	L1	
HPK3600066	77	BRIGHTON	2818	C4	
HPK3600067	78	ST CHARLES	2847	C4	
HPK3600068	79	GLEN OAKS	2863	C4	
HPK3600069	80	COVINGTON COVE	2875	C4	
HPK3600070	81	BARNARD HEIGHTS	2924	C4	
HPK3600071	82	EAST BENNINGTON PLACE	2927	C4	
HPK3600072	83	DELMONT	2937	C4	
HPK3600073	84	CLARENDON SPRINGS	2937	C4	
HPK3600074	85	WESTWOOD	2946	C4	
HPK3600075	86	DUNNINGTON	2946	C4	
HPK3600076	87	HAINESPORT	2947	C4	
HPK3600077	88	ARLINGTON HEIGHTS	2957	C4	
HPK3600078	89	CHANNING PLACE	3000	C4	
HPK3600079	90	EAST HAMPTON	3000	C4	
HPK3600080	91	GUILFORD CORNERS	3048	C4	
HPK3600081	92	NEWBERRY HEIGHTS	3059	C4	
HPK3600082	93	SUMMERVILLE	3110	L1	
HPK3600083	94	BRIAR VISTA	3148	L1	
HPK3600084	95	WINFIELD	3232	L1	
HPK3600085	96	AFTON VIEW	3250	L1	
HPK3600086	97	LEXINGTON HEIGHTS	3313	C4	
HPK3600087	98	WINCHESTER	3331	C4	
HPK3600088	99	COTSWOLD PLACE	3355	L1	
HPK3600089	100	NORWALK	3360	C4	YES
HPK3600090	101	WESSINGTON PLACE	3378	L1	
HPK3600091	102	SHELBURNE	3392	C4	
HPK3600092	103	TRENTON PLACE	3392	C4	
HPK3600093	104	PENDLETON PLACE	3394	C4	
HPK3600094	105	LENOX	3448	L1	
HPK3600095	106	GREENWOOD	3491	L1	
HPK3600096	107	FINLEY HILL	2800	C4	
HPK3600097	108	FOXBOROUGH HILL	2845	C4	
HPK3600098	109	218 HOLLY RIDGE	2860	C4	YES
HPK3600099	110	CALAVERAS	2860	C4	
HPK3600100	111	CHESTNUT LANE	2865	C4	YES

PLAN #	PAGE	PLAN NAME	SQUARE FOOTAGE	PRICE TIER	MATERIALS LIST
HPK3600101	112	225 HOLLY RIDGE	2898	C4	YES
HPK3600102	113	ANSLEY PARK HOME	2900	C4	
HPK3600103	114	WELCOME MEADOW	2919	C4	
HPK3600104	115	CAYMAN	2935	C4	
HPK3600105	116	FANCREST	2935	C4	YES
HPK3600106	117	WATERFORD	2935	C4	
HPK3600107	118	229 WILLOW TRACE	2996	C4	
HPK3600108	119	WELLINGTON	2998	C4	
HPK3600109	120	PROVIDENCE	3021	L1	
HPK3600110	121	ANDREAS	3021	L1	
HPK3600111	122	213 WILLOW TRACE	3043	C4	YES
HPK3600112	123	WALDEN	3045	L1	
HPK3600113	124	LAUREL LANE	3063	L1	
HPK3600114	125	MAGNOLIA PLACE	3104	L1	YES
HPK3600115	126	CUSHING MEADOWS	3159	L1	
HPK3600116	127	CORAL KEEP	3175	C4	
HPK3600117	128	CARA VISTA	3179	L1	
HPK3600118	129	AVALLON ESTATES	3196	L1	YES
HPK3600119	130	HIGHPOINT	3200	L1	YES
HPK3600120	131	DUNWOODY CLASSIC	3202	L1	YES
HPK3600121	132	230 MAGNOLIA PLACE	3227	L1	
HPK3600122	133	220 WILLOW TRACE	3245	L1	
HPK3600123	134	NORTH HIGHLANDS HOME	3248	L1	
HPK3600124	135	HERITAGE VIEW	3262	L1	
HPK3600125	136	SOUTHWIND	3285	L1	YES
HPK3600126	137	DRUID HILLS MANOR	3300	L1	YES
HPK3600127	138	139 KENNESAW COUNTRY	3342	L1	YES
HPK3600128	139	224 MAGNOLIA PLACE	3355	L1	YES
HPK3600129	140	343 WOODBURY	3367	L1	
HPK3600130	141	AVIGNON	3378	L1	
HPK3600131	142	STRATFORD PLACE	3387	L1	
HPK3600132	143	GRAYSON	3448	L1	
HPK3600133	144	PEACHTREE PLACE	3458	L1	YES
HPK3600134	145	CAMP HILL	3493	L1	
HPK3600135	146	LA MAISON DE REVES	4287	L2	
HPK3600136	150	CARRINGTON HILLS	3575	L1	
HPK3600137	151	SANTA ROSA CANYON	3576	L1	
HPK3600138	152	CANEY BRANCH	3650	L1	
HPK3600139	153	AMHERST	3695	L1	
HPK3600140	154	ST GERMAIN	3697	L1	
HPK3600141	155	HOLLY BLUFF	3700	L1	
HPK3600142	156	KENNSINGTON	3788	L1	
HPK3600143	157	MANVILLE COURT	3840	L1	
HPK3600144	158	BROADWINGS	3940	L1	YES
HPK3600145	159	NANTUCKET TRACE	4226	L2	
HPK3600146	160	CORDOVA PLACE	4246	L2	
HPK3600147	161	OXFORD HALL	4821	L2	
HPK3600148	162	BUCKINGHAM COURT	5073	L2	
HPK3600149	163	452 MANDERLEIGH	5130	L2	YES
HPK3600150	164	PEMBROKE HALL	5134	SQ7	
HPK3600151	165	BOURGOGNE	5193	L2	
HPK3600152	166	ROSEWOOD VILLA	5235	L2	
HPK3600153	167	AZALEA HALL	5814	SQ3	
HPK3600154	168	180 BRIDGEPORT PLANT	6061	L2	
HPK3600155	169	CUMBERLAND RIVER COTTAGE	3640	L1	
HPK3600156	170	YORKSHIRE	3730	L1	
HPK3600157	171	KENNESAW RIDGE	3951	L1	
HPK3600158	172	LEYLAND PLACE	4415	C4	
HPK3600159	173	BLYTHEWOOD	4168	L1	
HPK3600160	174	MEADOWVIEW	5412	L2	
HPK3600161	175	WOODMONT	4403	L2	
HPK3600162	176	ASHLAND GROVE	4271	L2	
HPK3600163	177	HAMSTEAD FARM	3606	L1	
HPK3600164	178	RALEIGH COURT	4278	L2	
HPK3600165	179	CLAIRMONT MANOR	4553	L2	
HPK3600166	180	COUNTRY CHICKERING	3761	L1	
HPK3600167	181	MILLSTEAD	3712	L1	